VOCABULARY CARTOONS II

Building an Educated
Vocabulary with
Sight and Sound
Memory Aids

Sam, Max, and Bryan Burchers

New Monic Books

Manufactured in the United States of America.
Library of Congress Catalog Card Number: 00-090409
ISBN: 0-9652422-6-9
Illustrations: Wally Littman, Lee Horton, David Horton, Bryan Burchers, & Gene Ostmark
Cover Design: Bryan Burchers, D.T. Publishing
Setup & Typography: Sam Burchers

Library of Congress Cataloging-in-Publication Data
Burchers, Sam
    Vocabulary Cartoons II, SAT Word Power
    Sam Burchers, Max Burchers, & Bryan Burchers
            p.   cm.
    Includes index.
    ISBN 0-9652422-6-9
    1. Vocabulary Cartoons II, SAT Word Power – United States.
II. Title
                        00-090409

New Monic Books
314-C Tamiami Trail
Punta Gorda, FL 33950
(941) 575-6669 $12.95

Acknowledgments

The Educators

Our gratitude to the following educators in Southwest Florida who had the foresight and initiative to introduce mnemonic cartoon test programs in their schools and classrooms. It was through their efforts that vocabulary cartoons have been proven to be a dynamic new technique in building a more educated vocabulary:

North Fort Myers High School
Ed Stickles, Princ.
Larry Marsh

Alva Middle School
Jerry Demming, Asst. Princ. Cur.
Jean Riner

Cape Coral High School
Karyl Davis, Asst. Princ. Cur.
Melisa Skinner
Sue Propert

Port Charlotte Middle School
Clyde Hoff, Princ.
Dianne Woolley

Mariner High School
Bonnie Hill, Asst. Princ. Cur.
Judy Baxley
Jennifer Basler
Sharon Kramer
Nancy Wiseman

Murdock Middle School
Lou Long, Princ.
Debbie Moore
William Valella

The Artists

Our special thanks to staff artists **Bryan Burchers**, **Wally Littman**, **Gene Ostmark**, **Lee Horton** and **Dave Horton**. Their collective talents provided the essential quality of zany humor and outrageous bizarreness that make cartoon mnemonics memorable.

Contributing Writer/Editor

A special thanks to **Sue Propert** for contributing her time and talent. Her attention to detail greatly enhanced the quality of this book.

Contents

Introduction

About Vocabulary Cartoons I

First published in 1996, *Vocabulary Cartoons, SAT Word Power* was intended to be our only vocabulary book. Shortly thereafter, teachers began using our book in their classrooms with great success. Educators were impressed with the ease and proficiency at which their students were learning new words. Many were learning two to three times more words than students using traditional rote memory vocabulary books. By 1998 *Vocabulary Cartoons, SAT Word Power* had become Ingram's (the USA's largest retail book distributor) best selling vocabulary book in the nation*. Encouraged with the success of our first book, we set out to write a series of Vocabulary Cartoon books using the same mnemonic format.

Vocabulary Cartoons, Elementary Edition

Due to the demand for a lower level vocabulary book, we published *Vocabulary Cartoons, Elementary Edition* in 1998. Used primarily in 3rd through 6th grades, the *Elementary Edition* soon gained recognition similar to our first book. In addition, middle and high schools soon began using this book with their challenged students. Accordingly, the "Elementary Edition" title was taken off the cover so it could more easily be used in both primary and secondary schools without offending non-elementary students.

*Source: Ingram Book Company

Vocabulary Cartoons II, SAT Word Power

The book you are now reading, *Vocabulary Cartoons II, SAT Word Power*, picks up where SAT I leaves off. It also contains 290 words commonly found in national SAT tests. In verbal difficulty, the words in this edition are equal to the words found in *Vocabulary Cartoons I*.

Brain-Friendly Learning With Vocabulary Mnemonics

In recent years neuroscientists have uncovered astonishing facts about how the brain learns, stores, and retrieves information! The use of mnemonic applications is high on the list of the way the brain learns most naturally and efficiently. Vocabulary Cartoon mnemonic strategies not only accelerate learning, but they also motivate, entertain, and build self-esteem!

Vocabulary Cartoons and How They Work

Vocabulary Cartoons consist of both rhymes and humorous cartoons that employ proven mnemonic techniques into the vocabulary learning experience. All mnemonics are based on association, the idea being to associate what you are trying to remember with something you already know.

Rhymes and Jingles are effective memory aids. Linking rhyming words to words you already know is classic mnemonic methodology. Who in America does not know the date America was discovered by the jingle, "Columbus Sailed The Ocean Blue?"

Visual Images in the form of humorous cartoons make up the second mnemonic. Anything that can be visualized is easier to remember. The more bizarre or outrageous the cartoon, the easier it is to remember.

Who Would Most Benefit From This Book?

Vocabulary Cartoons are designed for anyone wishing to build a stronger vocabulary. However, *Vocabulary Cartoons* are particularly recommended for students studying for Pre-Scholastic Aptitude Tests (P.S.A.T.), Scholastic Aptitude Tests (S.A.T.) and Graduate Record Exams (G.R.E.); it is also suitable for older students in Adult Education courses, English as a Second Language (E.S.O.L.) students; those in Exceptional Student Education (E.S.E.) programs and Attention Deficit Disorder (A.D.D.) programs.

School Test Results

The effectiveness of *Vocabulary Cartoons* as a faster, easier learning tool for all types of students has been established in six independent school tests in Southwest Florida. These tests took place in 1995 and 1996 and involved hundreds of students at different grade levels.

In Port Charlotte Middle School, Mrs. Woolley's eighth grade class scored 180% higher test grades with *Vocabulary Cartoon* study books than did the control class that had rote memory study books.

At Cape Coral High School, English teacher Melissa Skinner's tenth grade class using *Vocabulary Cartoons* scored 105% higher, and had six times more "A's" than did the control tenth grade class without the *Vocabulary Cartoon* books.

In Larry Marsh's ninth grade English classes at North

Fort Myers High, fifty-five ninth grade students learned an average of 147 new words with only three hours of study. Some students learned more than one new word for every study minute.

Altogether, in double blind tests, students using *Vocabulary Cartoons* scored an average 72% higher grades than did the control students using rote memory study books.

Vocabulary Cartoons are not intended to replace traditional vocabulary study books. However, they are a valuable building block as well as an adjunct to the overall vocabulary learning process.

How To Use This Book

Each page consists of five elements:

1. The **main word**. This is the word to be learned. It is followed by the phonetic pronunciation and a definition.

> *ACCRUE (ah KROO), v. to increase or accumulate over time*

2. The **link word**. The link word is a simple word (or words) which rhymes or sounds like the main word.

> *Link: A CREW*

3. The **caption**. The caption connects the main word and the linking word in a mnemonic rhyme.

> *"Pirates know how to ACCRUE A CREW."*

4. The **cartoon**. The caption underscores a bizarre or humorous cartoon which incorporates the main word and the linking word into a visual mnemonic.

"Pirates know how to ACCRUE A CREW."

Once you make the word association between *ACCRUE* and *A CREW*, whenever you hear the word "*ACCRUE*," the linking words "*A CREW*" will come to mind to remind you of "*A CREW* being *ACCRUED*.*"*

Use the book like flash cards, flipping through the cartoons one by one a chapter at a time. Soon you will find that the main word and its associating sound-like word link together. At about this time, the cartoon mnemonic becomes fixed in the mind's eye, and the mnemonic process is complete!

The words selected as *Vocabulary Cartoons II* are those frequently found on the S.A.T. and G.R.E. How well you do on the verbal skill sections of either test is almost exclusively determined by your vocabulary skills.

Remember that approximately 90% of university courses require reading comprehension. A good reader must have an extensive vocabulary.

COPIOUS
(KOH pee us) *adj.*
abundant; plentiful
Link: CUP

"A COPIOUS CUP of coffee."

- ❏ Farmer Brown was overjoyed with his COPIOUS crop of tomatoes.

- ❏ David gave COPIOUS reasons why he should be allowed to stay home from school.

- ❏ Professor Lang always gave COPIOUS notes in history class.

TENACIOUS

(teh NAY shus) *adj.*

tough; stubborn; not letting go

Link: TENNIS ACES

"TENNIS ACES are TENACIOUS."

- ❑ David's TENACITY paid-off and finally won him the job he wanted. (To be TENACIOUS is to have TENACITY.)

- ❑ Susan's TENACIOUS efforts to learn English won her the admiration of her teacher.

- ❑ The weeds in our lawn are so TENACIOUS we can never get rid of them.

SURREPTITIOUS
(sur ep TISH us) *adj.*
done or acting in a secret, sly manner
Link: SUSPICIOUS

*"To escape from the circus, an elephant has to be
SURREPTITIOUS without being SUSPICIOUS."*

- Ray was SURREPTITIOUS in his approach to the
  campground so he was able to take everyone by
  surprise.

- Helen SURREPTITIOUSLY crept around the car,
  hoping to get the cat out from under it.

- The magician was so SURREPTITIOUS during his
  magic trick that the audience was completely
  fooled.

VORACIOUS

(vo RAY shus) *adj.*

an insatiable appetite for an activity or pursuit;
eager to consume great amounts of food

Link: **GOOD GRACIOUS**

"GOOD GRACIOUS, what VORACIOUS fish."

- ❑ The dog's VORACIOUS appetite could not be satisfied with small treats.

- ❑ To Captain Ahab, Moby Dick seems like a VORACIOUS mammal.

- ❑ Teenage boys tend to be VORACIOUS eaters.

OFFICIOUS
(uh FISH us) *adj.*
ready to serve; eager in offering
unwanted services or advice
Link: OFFICE

"An OFFICIOUS OFFICE helper."

❑ Uncle Dan was so OFFICIOUS that he wanted to help me work on my antique cars even though he knew nothing about engines.

❑ The OFFICIOUS waitress would not go away even when Jennifer told her that she wanted only coffee.

❑ Ralph's OFFICIOUSNESS was an attempt to make friends which usually backfired on him.

SPURIOUS

(SPYUUR ee us) *adj.*

not genuine; false

Link: SPURS

"SPURIOUS SPURS."

- ❑ The politician made SPURIOUS claims about his opponent's views of labor reform.

- ❑ The police discovered cheap items which were carrying expensive labels being SPURIOUSLY manufactured in an illegal operation in the city.

- ❑ An expert was called in to examine the antiques for SPURIOUSNESS.

ONEROUS
(AHN ur us) *adj.*
troublesome or oppressive;
burdensome
Link: OWNER

"A pet shop OWNER'S life can become ONEROUS."

- ❑ Our platoon was given the ONEROUS duty of charging up a well-defended hill.

- ❑ After our truck ran out of gas, we had the ONEROUS task of pushing it two miles to the nearest gas station.

- ❑ The teacher was given a classroom aide because her class was so ONEROUS.

GREGARIOUS

(gruh GAIR ee us) *adj.*
seeking and enjoying the company
of others; sociable

Link: **GREG HILARIOUS**

*"GREGARIOUS GREG
was HILARIOUS."*

❑ Paige was so GREGARIOUS she hated to be alone.

❑ Carol, to the contrary, was not GREGARIOUS. At parties she rarely talked with anyone.

❑ Bernard's GREGARIOUS nature made him an enjoyable person.

PIOUS
(PI us) *adj.*
devout or virtuous; holy
Link: **PIE**

"A PIOUS PIE."

❏ Elizabeth PIOUSLY said her prayers every night before bed.

❏ The prisoner's speech on honesty showed a PIOUS disregard for his own dishonesty.

❏ The opposite of PIOUS is IMPIOUS, meaning lacking in reverence or respect.

SCRUPULOUS

(SKROO pyu les) *adj.*
careful of small details; honest;
conscientious

Link: **SCREWS**

*"Aircraft manufacturers must be SCRUPULOUS with
the placement of SCREWS."*

❑ Because his parents are such SCRUPULOUS
people, Jim knew the difference between right
and wrong even as a small boy.

❑ President Abraham Lincoln is known for his
SCRUPULOUSNESS.

❑ The clerk SCRUPULOUSLY followed the man to
his car to give him the change he had forgotten.

REVIEW #1: Match the word with its definition.

1. copious – (cup)
2. tenacious – (tennis ace)
3. surreptitious – (suspicious)
4. voracious – (good gracious)
5. officious – (office)
6. spurious – (spurs)
7. onerous – (owner)
8. gregarious – (Greg hilarious)
9. pious – (pie)
10. scrupulous – (screws)

a. troublesome
b. acting in a secret manner
c. careful of small details
d. devout or virtuous
e. tough; stubborn
f. sociable
g. abundant; plentiful
h. offering unwanted advice
i. an insatiable appetite
j. false

Fill in the blanks with the appropriate word. The word form may need changing.

1. Teenage boys tend to be _____ eaters.

2. Our platoon was given the _____ duty of charging up a well defended hill.

3. Because his parents are such _____ people, Jim knew the difference between right and wrong even as a small boy.

4. The _____ waitress would not go away even when Jennifer told her that she wanted only coffee.

5. Paige was so _____ she hated to be alone.

6. Helen _____ crept around the car, hoping to get the cat out from under it.

7. Farmer Brown was overjoyed with his _____ crop of tomatoes.

8. Elizabeth _____ said her prayers every night before bed.

9. The weeds in our lawn are so _____ we could never get rid of them.

10. The politician made _____ claims about his opponent's views of labor reform.

ATTRITION

(ah TRISH un) *n.*
a gradual reduction or weakening;
a rubbing away
Link: **FISHIN'**

"Over-FISHIN' can lead to ATTRITION."

❏ The war became a battle of ATTRITION, each side wearing down the other.

❏ Because our school has so many older teachers, the ATTRITION rate is high.

❏ Washed ashore, the once jagged piece of glass had become a smoothed gem due to the ATTRITION of the sea and sand.

EDIFICATION
(ED ih fih kay shun) *n.*
enlighten; instruct
Link: ED ON VACATION

*"ED getting some EDIFICATION while
on VACATION."*

❏ Many parents send their children to Sunday School for moral EDIFICATION.

❏ Etiquette is an important part of one's social EDIFICATION.

❏ We would have been lost at the art show had not programs been provided for our EDIFICATION.

ABLUTION

(ah BLOO shun) *n.*

a cleansing with water or other liquid, especially as a religious ritual; the liquid used in such an act

Link: **SOLUTION**

"The SOLUTION to baby's ABLUTION."

- ☐ The priest performed his ABLUTIONS in private.

- ☐ The witch doctor used ABLUTIONS of clear water to cleanse the stricken man of his illness.

- ☐ The ABLUTIONARY water seemed to help the suffering woman.

ELOCUTION
(el oh KYOO shun) *n.*
the art of public speaking
Link: **EXECUTION**

*"ELOCUTION is a good way to
postpone an EXECUTION."*

- ❑ Classes in ELOCUTION are helpful to those who seek a career in politics.

- ❑ The Greek orator Demosthenes had a speech impediment, but he taught himself proper ELOCUTION by reciting poetry.

- ❑ Mark Twain was known for his ELOCUTION as well as his stories.

WRITHE

(ryth) *v.*

to cause to twist or bend; to suffer
acutely, as in pain or embarrassment

Link: **RIDE**

"Wild horses WRITHE when cowboys RIDE."

❑ The fish WRITHED free of the hook and escaped
back into the sea.

❑ Some forms of dance make it look as though the
dancer is WRITHING in pain.

❑ Tina WRITHED when the class heard she had
failed chemistry for the third time.

PEDESTRIAN
(peh DES tree ahn) *adj.*
ordinary; moving on foot
Link: **PEDESTRIAN**

"PEDESTRIAN PEDESTRIANS."

❑ Most of the villages in the Andes Mountains have PEDESTRIAN traffic.

❑ For once, can't we do something that isn't so boringly PEDESTRIAN?

❑ The right frame can make a PEDESTRIAN painting look like a million bucks.

CARRION
(KAIR ee un) *n.*
dead and rotting flesh
Link: **CARRY ON**

"CARRION CARRY ON luggage."

- ❏ After mauling its prey, the lion left the CARRION to the hyenas.
- ❏ Days after the battle, the battlefield was littered by the CARRION of brave soldiers.
- ❏ CARRION is a vulture's main source of food.

PINION
(PIN yun) *n.*
bind the wings so as not to fly;
confine
Link: PIN

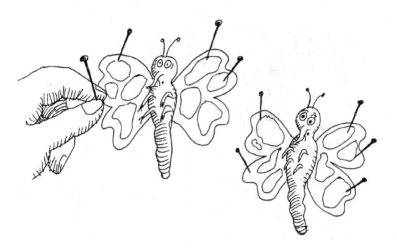

"The PINS PINIONED the wings."

❑ The handcuffs were used to PINION his hands.

❑ He was PINIONED to the stake by his captors.

❑ Jake had PINIONED John to the wall before someone could stop the altercation.

KISMET
(KIZ met) *n.*
fate
Link: **KISS ME**

"KISS ME baby, it's KISMET."

- ❑ The happy couple attributed the success of their relationship to KISMET.

- ❑ To those who believe in fate, KISMET is the cause of everything.

- ❑ It was KISMET that they both returned to their old high school on the same day twenty years after graduation.

AMBIVALENCE

(am BIV ah lents) *n.*
indecision; experiencing
contradictory emotions
Link: **AMBULANCE**

"AMBIVALENCE between two AMBULANCES."

- ❏ Jim's AMBIVALENCE toward his boss made him regret the day he accepted the job.

- ❏ Farmer Brown was AMBIVALENT about whether to plant tomatoes or corn.

- ❏ Jeb's AMBIVALENCE about which diet to choose made him disregard the whole idea of losing weight.

REVIEW #2: Match the word with its definition.

1. attrition – (fishin')
2. edification – (Ed on vacation)
3. ablution – (solution)
4. elocution – (execution)
5. writhe – (ride)
6. pedestrian – (pedestrian)
7. carrion – (carry on)
8. pinion – (pin)
9. kismet – (kiss me)
10. ambivalence – (ambulance)

a. to cause to twist or bend
b. a cleansing
c. fate
d. rotting flesh
e. a gradual reduction
f. the art of public speaking
g. indecision
h. enlighten; instruct
i. confine
j. ordinary

Fill in the blanks with the appropriate word. The word form may need changing.

1. The fish _____ free of the hook and escaped back into the sea.

2. John's _____ about which diet to choose made him disregard the whole idea of losing weight.

3. Many parents send their children to Sunday School for moral _____.

4. Classes in _____ are helpful to those who seek a career in politics.

5. The happy couple attributed the success of their relationship to _____.

6. The witch doctor used _____ of clear water to cleanse the stricken man of his illness.

7. Days after the battle, the battlefield was littered by the _____ of brave soldiers.

8. The right frame can make a _____ painting look like a million bucks.

9. The handcuffs were used to _____ his hands.

10. The war became a battle of _____, each side wearing down the other.

36

DEPLOY
(di PLOY) *v.*
to arrange strategically
Link: TOY

"David DEPLOYED his TOYS to attack his sister."

- The general's intelligent DEPLOYMENT of his troops along the eastern front won the battle.

- The admiral DEPLOYED his ships at the entrance to the harbor.

- By DEPLOYING all his resources, Phil was able to buy the car.

CAVALIER

(kav ah LEER) *adj.*
casual; carefree and nonchalant; arrogant
disregard; *n.* a gallant gentleman
Link: **CAVALRY**

*"Colonel Jones was CAVALIER with
his CAVALRY troops."*

❑ We could all tell before the wedding that Phil had
a CAVALIER attitude toward marriage.

❑ Colonel Moore was disliked because of his
CAVALIER attitude toward the troops in his
command.

❑ Darren was so CAVALIER that he always kissed a
lady's hand when first introduced.

EGG
(eg) *v.*
to encourage or incite to action
Link: EGG

"Humpty was EGGED to jump."

❑ The bully EGGED the little boy to fight until he cried.

❑ My friends EGGED me to try out for the tennis team.

❑ Without the crowd EGGING me on, I don't think I could have finished running the marathon.

METE

(MEET) *v.*

to distribute by or as if by measure; allot

Link: **MEAT**

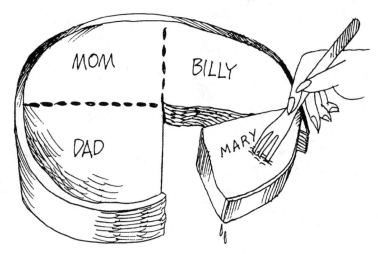

"Mom always METES out the MEAT."

- ❑ Allison stood in the doorway in a witch costume and METED out Halloween candy to all the kids.

- ❑ The volunteer fireman METED out sandbags to all worried homeowners.

- ❑ The sergeant METED out ammunition to all soldiers in the platoon.

NULLIFY
(NUL ih fy) *v.*
to make useless; cancel; undo
Link: **FLY**

"How to NULLIFY a FLY."

- ❏ Christopher said his agreement to play for the Cowboys had been NULLIFIED due to his injury.

- ❏ The purchase contract could be NULLIFIED because it had never been signed by the buyer.

- ❏ Jane wanted her marriage ANNULLED because her husband was trying to NULLIFY their prenuptial agreement.

41

EMBROIL

(im BROYL) *v.*
to involve in argument or hostile
action; to throw in disorder
Link: BOIL

"The lobster preferred EMBROILING to BOILING."

❑ Most of the civilized world was EMBROILED in
conflict during World War II.

❑ The attorneys were EMBROILED in caustic
argument.

❑ An EMBROILING situation arose when the rock
concert was cancelled.

WAFFLE
(WOF ul) *v.*
to speak or write evasively
Link: WAFFLE

"A WAFFLE WAFFLING the questions."

☐ When asked by the journalist if he felt he was deserving of the Oscar, the actor WAFFLED his reply since he knew he had done very little real acting.

☐ The president knew he would need to WAFFLE some of the questions the press would ask about the scandal surrounding his administration.

☐ Speech writers make a living WAFFLING the issues.

ASCRIBE

(ah SKRYBE) *v.*
to attribute to a specific cause,
source, or origin

Link: **TRIBE**

*"Why the TRIBE ASCRIBED the nickname
'Long Nose' to the cavalry."*

- ❑ The physics professor ASCRIBES to the theory that what goes up must come down.

- ❑ Samantha ASCRIBED her weight loss to a diet of fruits and vegetables.

- ❑ Kurt ASCRIBED his gold medal to hard work and dedication.

ENHANCE
(en HANS) *v.*
to improve; to intensify
Link: **DANCE**

*"The band thought new speakers would
ENHANCE the DANCE music."*

❑ Sheila believed applying a lot of makeup would
ENHANCE her looks; when in reality it made her
look like a clown.

❑ Bob ENHANCED his race car's performance by
installing a more powerful engine.

❑ Since ENHANCING my computer's modem, I am
able to do research more quickly.

IMPAIR

(im PAIR) *v.*
to cause to diminish, as in
strength, value, or quality

Link: **PEAR**

"An IMPAIRED PEAR."

- ❑ A constant fast-food diet will eventually IMPAIR one's health.

- ❑ An overly aggressive negotiator can often IMPAIR negotiations.

- ❑ Our best soccer player was IMPAIRED when he hurt his knee.

REVIEW #3: Match the word with its definition.

1. deploy – (toy)
2. cavalier – (cavalry)
3. egg – (egg)
4. mete – (meat)
5. nullify – (fly)
6. embroil – (boil)
7. waffle – (waffle)
8. ascribe – (tribe)
9. enhance – (dance)
10. impair – (pear)

a. to encourage
b. to cancel; undo
c. to arrange strategically
d. to distribute
e. to attribute to a specific cause
f. to improve or intensify
g. to throw in disorder
h. to diminish in quality
i. casual; carefree
j. to speak or write evasively

Fill in the blanks with the appropriate word. The word form may need changing.

1. Most of the civilized world was _____ in conflict during World War II.

2. We could tell before the wedding that Phil had a _____ attitude toward marriage.

3. Samantha _____ her weight loss to a diet of fruits and vegetables.

4. Sheila believed applying a lot of makeup would _____ her appearance.

5. The admiral _____ his ships at the entrance to the harbor.

6. A constant fast-food diet will eventually _____ one's health.

7. The sergeant _____ out ammunition to all soldiers in the platoon.

8. The president knew he would need to _____ some of the questions the press would ask about the scandal surrounding the administration.

9. The purchase contract could be _____ because it had never been signed by the buyer.

10. The bully _____ the little boy to fight until he cried.

TERSE

(turs) *adj.*

brief and to the point; concise

Link: VERSE

"*A TERSE Shakespearean VERSE.*"

- ❑ Rich could tell he had annoyed his teacher when she gave him a TERSE reply.

- ❑ Hemingway is best known for his TERSE style of writing.

- ❑ When Sally becomes annoyed and wants to make her point, she becomes very TERSE.

COERCE
(koh URS) *v.*
to force someone by threatening or
physically overpowering him
Link: **HORSE**

"COERCING a HORSE."

- ❏ The burglar's confession was COERCED by the police.

- ❏ Elizabeth was COERCED by her sister to take another cookie from the jar.

- ❏ It was evident from the video tape that the hostage was COERCED to lie about the status of her condition.

49

DIVERSE
(di VURS) *adj.*
different; varied
Link: **DIVERS**

"DIVERSE sky DIVERS."

❑ Humphrey had a DIVERSE collection of classic automobiles.

❑ The California Gold Rush attracted people of DIVERSE backgrounds: farmers, bankers and tradesmen made the journey to the gold fields.

❑ Randy had a DIVERSE education with degrees in medicine, law, and business.

ABATE
(ah BAIT) *v.*
to reduce
Link: **BAIT**

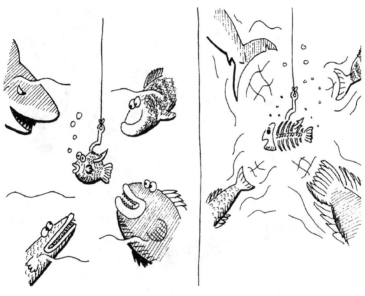

"ABATED BAIT."

☐ Marta's defeat in the tennis tournament did not ABATE her zeal for the game.

☐ Tom went to a financial consultant to seek advice on ABATING his burdening debts.

☐ When the storm finally ABATED, we resumed our family picnic.

ABIDE
(ah BYDE) *v.*
to remain; continue; stay; endure
Link: SIDE

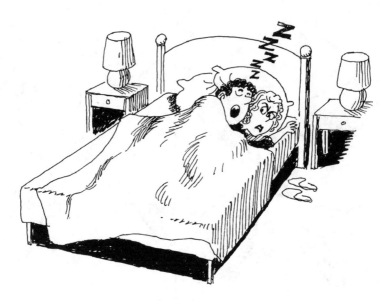

*"Ron could not ABIDE by staying
on his SIDE of the bed."*

❑ The prisoner knew he had to ABIDE by the
verdict of the jury.

❑ Josh's father always told him if he made a
promise, he must ABIDE by it.

❑ Soldiers in battle need to have an ABIDING faith
in their fellow soldiers.

GAMBIT

(GAM bit) *v.*

to take a risk for some advantage

Link: GAMBLE

"A GAMBIT not worth the GAMBLE."

❑ The general's GAMBIT paid off when his troops won the battle.

❑ The chess player's GAMBIT was unsuccessful when he was put in checkmate.

❑ The employee's daring GAMBIT won him a raise from his boss.

JAUNT
(jawnt) *n.*
a short pleasure trip
Link: **HAUNT**

"A JAUNT HAUNT."

- ❑ After not taking a family vacation for two years, a JAUNT to the beach was a pleasant respite.

- ❑ My parents are always taking JAUNTS in their new motor home.

- ❑ Mary and Bryan always enjoy their annual JAUNT to the mountains.

FRANK

(frangk) *adj.*

straightforward; open and sincere in expression

Link: **FRANKFURTER**

"A FRANK FRANKFURTER."

- ❑ Jim's FRANK remark about Marge's weight made her cry.

- ❑ The doctor was FRANK about Lisa's prognosis.

- ❑ The boss encouraged us to speak FRANKLY at the meeting.

LITHE
(lythe) *adj.*
bending easily and gracefully
Link: **LIZA**

"LIZA is the most LITHE gymnast on our team."

❏ The LITHE ballerina stretched her muscles before her performance.

❏ The gymnast was so LITHESOME that she dismounted without a sound.

❏ The dancer was as LITHE as a cat as he leapt across the stage.

AESTHETIC

(es THET ik) *adj.*
having to do with artistic beauty
Link: ATHLETIC

"An AESTHETIC ATHLETE."

❑ Japanese rock gardens demonstrate AESTHETIC values typical of a Far Eastern culture.

❑ The artist had an uncanny sense of AESTHETICS; he could make a drawing of a plate of food look like a Thanksgiving feast.

❑ Jeannie molded the ugly lump of clay into an AESTHETICALLY pleasing masterpiece.

REVIEW #4: Match the word with its definition.

1. terse – (verse)
2. coerce – (horse)
3. diverse – (divers)
4. abate – (bait)
5. abide – (side)
6. gambit – gamble
7. jaunt – (haunt)
8. frank – (frankfurter)
9. lithe – (Liza)
10. aesthetic – (athletic)

a. a short pleasure trip
b. concise
c. to remain; continue; stay
d. to take a risk
e. to reduce
f. bending easily
g. different; varied
h. to force someone by threatening
i. having to do with artistic beauty
j. straightforward

Fill in the blanks with the appropriate word. The word form may need changing.

1. The prisoner knew he had to _____ by the verdict of the jury.

2. Humphrey had a _____ collection of classic automobiles.

3. Hemingway is best known for his _____ style of writing.

4. The doctor was _____ about Melissa's prognosis.

5. The chess player's _____ was unsuccessful when he was put in checkmate.

6. The dancer was as _____ as a cat as he leapt across the stage.

7. The burglar's confession was _____ by the police.

8. Mary and Bryan always enjoy their annual _____ to the mountains.

9. When the storm finally _____, we resumed our family picnic.

10. Japanese rock gardens demonstrate _____ values typical of a Far Eastern culture.

GULLIBLE
(GUL ih bul) *adj.*
easily cheated or fooled
Link: GULL

"A GULLIBLE GULL."

- ❑ Joel could not believe he had been so GULLIBLE as to believe his friend's wild story.

- ❑ Con artists rely on the GULLIBILITY of people to take money from their victims.

- ❑ The elderly woman GULLIBLY gave her credit card number to the man on the phone.

MAWKISH
(MAW kish) *adj.*
excessively and objectionably sentimental
Link: **MA'S KISS**

"MA'S KISS can be MAWKISH."

❑ Elizabeth is so MAWKISH that she cries at every wedding.

❑ Steve doesn't care for MAWKISH birthday cards; he likes funny ones instead.

❑ The bride's MAWKISH behavior embarrassed the groom.

RAFFISH

(RAF ish) *adj.*
cheaply vulgar in appearance or
nature; tawdry; disreputable
Link: FISH

"A RAFFISH FISH."

- ❏ The RAFFISH character had been seen at the murder and was taken in for questioning.

- ❏ RAFFISHLY dressed, the movie star was out of place at a country picnic.

- ❏ Because of his RAFFISHNESS, the authorities escorted him from the stadium.

CONTINUUM

(kun TIN yoo um) *n.*
a continuous whole without clear
division into parts
Link: CONTINUE

*"A beam of light is a CONTINUUM which
CONTINUES from its source."*

❏ A spectrum of light is a CONTINUUM into which each color blends with its neighbors.

❏ At the carnival, a CONTINUUM of weaving dances moved in a seemingly endless chain.

❏ Albert Einstein believed that space and time are not distinct dimensions, but a CONTINUUM, which he called the Theory of Relativity.

TRAVAIL
(tre VAYL) *n.*
strenuous physical or mental labor
or effort; the labor of childbirth
Link: **TRAIL**

*"Much TRAVAIL was required crossing
the Oregon TRAIL."*

- ☐ Modern medicine has helped lessen the TRAVAIL of childbirth.

- ☐ When he saw his flourishing crops, he realized his TRAVAIL had been worth it.

- ☐ Her face showed the lines of her TRAVAIL with cancer.

INTREPID

(in TREP id) *adj.*

fearless; bold

Link: **TRIP ED**

"Everyone considered David INTREPID after he TRIPPED ED, the bully, in the cafeteria."

- ❏ The bullfighter was INTREPID as he stood in the arena before the fierce bull.

- ❏ Ed INTREPIDLY opened the hatch of the plane as he prepared for his first jump.

- ❏ The Green Berets have always been known for their INTREPIDITY.

LANGUID
(LANG gwid) *adj.*
lacking energy; weak; showing
little interest in anything
Link: SQUID

"A LANGUID SQUID."

❑ After his bout with the flu, Joe was LANGUID and unable to workout for over a week.

❑ Jill finished the triathlon, but at the finish line she LANGUIDLY sank to the ground.

❑ The teacher's LANGUID approach to American History did not motivate the class.

EXODUS
(EK suh dus) *n.*
a mass departure
Link: EXIT BUS

"A BUS EXODUS from the rear EXIT."

- ❏ There was an immediate EXODUS of the theater when someone yelled, "Fire!"

- ❏ After the hurricane evacuation was announced, there was mass EXODUS of people from the town.

- ❏ The forest fire created an EXODUS of animals.

INFLUX
(IN fluks) *n.*
a mass arrival or incoming;
a continuous coming
Link: **TRUCKS**

"An INFLUX of TRUCKS."

- ❑ South Florida has an INFLUX of northern tourists every winter.

- ❑ The INFLUX of peoples of other countries during the seventeenth and eighteenth centuries is what made America a melting pot.

- ❑ We will have to build an addition on to the school because of the INFLUX of new students.

ABASH

(ah BASH) *v.*

to make ashamed or uneasy

Link: **CASH**

*"Tony was ABASH when he discovered
he had no CASH."*

❑ Caught listening to her sister's conversation, Jen was ABASH and quickly put down the receiver.

❑ Joe was not at all ABASHED when he opened a valentine from Linda.

❑ Nate UNABASHEDLY mopped up the table after he spilled his milk.

REVIEW #5: Match the word with its definition.

1. gullible – (gull)
2. mawkish – (ma's kiss)
3. raffish – (fish)
4. continuum – (continue)
5. travail – (travel)
6. intrepid – (trip Ed)
7. languid – (squid)
8. exodus – (exit bus)
9. influx – (trucks)
10. abash – (cash)

a. fearless, bold
b. a mass departure
c. lacking energy
d. excessively sentimental
e. to make ashamed
f. strenuous physical effort
g. a continuous whole
h. easily cheated or fooled
i. a mass arrival
j. cheaply vulgar in appearance

Fill in the blanks with the appropriate word. The word form may need changing.

1. Caught listening to her sister's conversation, Jen was _____ and quickly put down the receiver.

2. Joel could not believe he had been so _____ as to believe his friend's wild story.

3. Modern medicine has helped lessen the _____ of childbirth.

4. The _____ character had been seen at the murder and was taken in for questioning.

5. There was an immediate _____ of the theater when someone yelled, "Fire!".

6. South Florida has an _____ of northern tourists every winter.

7. Mary is so _____ that she cries at every wedding.

8. A spectrum of light is a _____ which each color blends with its neighbors.

9. The teacher's _____ approach to American History did not motivate the class.

10. The bullfighter was _____ as he stood in the arena before the fierce bull.

INCESSANT

(in SES unt) *adj.*
continuing without interruption;
nonstop

Link: **INSECTS AND ANTS**

*"INSECTS and ANTS are INCESSANT
picnic pests."*

- ❑ The teacher gave Allison and Karen a detention for their INCESSANT chatter in class.

- ❑ The INCESSANT rain flooded the front yard.

- ❑ Their INCESSANT bickering drove Mike and Barbara to divorce.

LATENT
(LAYT nt) *adj.*
laying hidden or undeveloped;
potential
Link: **LAY TENT**

"Never LAY your TENT on a LATENT volcano."

- ❑ Trent had a LATENT talent as a singer which he didn't discover until he was in his 50's.

- ❑ Because the disease was in a LATENT state, no one knew she was ill.

- ❑ Jeri's parents were unaware of her LATENT desire to study law and to become an attorney.

ELOQUENT

(EL oh kwent) *adj.*
extremely expressive in speech,
writing, or movement
Link: **ELEPHANT**

EVERYONE PARTISON TO THIS MAGNIFICENT CRUSADE AGAINST IVORY POACHERS MUST MAKE A PRODIGOUS EFFORT IN SUPPORT OF OUR NOBLE CAUSE.

"An ELOQUENT ELEPHANT"

❑ Stan gave a moving, ELOQUENT speech.

❑ Shakespeare's plays are very ELOQUENTLY written.

❑ As the queen approached, the knight responded with an ELOQUENT bow.

DIFFIDENT

(DIF ih dent) *adj.*
lacking self-confidence; timid
Link: **DIFFERENT**

*"Is Lord Wellington DIFFIDENT about
swimming or is he DIFFERENT?"*

❑ The DIFFIDENT boy always sat alone in the cafeteria.

❑ In order to assuage her DIFFIDENCE, Beth was persuaded to enroll in drama class.

❑ The DIFFIDENT kitten was stuck up in the tree for hours.

MALCONTENT

(mal kon TENT) *adj.*
dissatisfied with existing conditions
Link: CONTENT

*"Once a MALCONTENT, the prisoner was now
CONTENT with his living conditions."*

❏ The labor strikers were MALCONTENTS who
did not even work at the company.

❏ We seem to always have one MALCONTENT
who can negatively impact team spirit.

❏ Roger, a MALCONTENT, was asked to resign
before he caused further problems.

EMINENT
(EM ih nent) *adj.*
standing out, renowned;
distinguished; prominent
Link: **EMMA'S TENT**

"EMMA'S TENT was the most EMINENT of the girl scouts tents."

❏ Michael Jordan is considered one of the most EMINENT basketball players of the 20th century.

❏ The most EMINENT feature of the hammerhead shark is its hammer-shaped head.

❏ The audience fell silent when the EMINENT singer walked on stage.

WINCE

(wints) *v.*
to flinch; to shrink back or start
aside, as from a blow or pain
Link: PRINCE

*"The PRINCE WINCED when he slipped on
Cinderella's glass slipper."*

❑ When she saw her test score, she WINCED at the
thought of having to show it to her parents.

❑ Certain sounds, like the scratching of fingernails
on chalk boards, seem to make most people
WINCE.

❑ The puppy WINCED when the man tried to pet
it.

PRUDENT
(PROOD ent) *adj.*
cautious; discreet; exercising
good judgment
Link: **STUDENT**

*"A PRUDENT STUDENT prepares ahead
for her math test."*

❑ The PRUDENT stock broker was willing to make investment suggestions that carried little risk.

❑ My mother PRUDENTLY guided me through some very difficult times.

❑ Michele decided it would be PRUDENT to ignore the insult and to walk away from such a hateful girl.

AUGMENT
(awg MENT) *v.*
to make or become greater
Link: **CEMENT**

*"How not to AUGMENT a driveway
with CEMENT."*

- ❑ The king attempted to AUGMENT his army by going into villages and drafting men into service.

- ❑ Jack's part time job did little to AUGMENT his family's financial woes.

- ❑ The President AUGMENTED his problems by denying his involvement in any wrong doing.

EBULLIENCE
(i BUUL yents) *n.*
enthusiastic; bubbling with excitement
Link: BULL DANCE

"EBULLIENCE at the BULL DANCE."

❑ Chris's EBULLIENT personality won her many friends.

❑ Joan's EBULLIENCE for her work is obvious in her time and effort.

❑ Of the two brothers, Ed is the more EBULLIENT, while Tom is more staid.

REVIEW #6: Match the word with its definition.

1. incessant – (insects and ants)
2. latent – (lay tent)
3. eloquent – (elephant)
4. diffident – (different)
5. malcontent – (content)
6. eminent – (Emma's tent)
7. wince – (prince)
8. prudent – (student)
9. augment – (cement)
10. ebullience – (bull dance)

a. to flinch
b. to make greater
c. nonstop
d. timid
e. dissatisfied with existing conditions
f. standing out
g. enthusiastic
h. cautious
i. expressive in speech, writing, or movement
j. laying hidden

Fill in the blanks with the appropriate word. The word form may need changing.

1. Trent had a _____ talent as a singer which he didn't discover until he was in his 50's.

2. Michael Jordan is considered one of the most _____ basketball players of the 20th century.

3. The teacher gave Allison and Karen a detention for their _____ chatter in class.

4. The puppy _____ when the man tried to pet it.

5. The _____ stock broker was willing to make investment suggestions that carried little risk.

6. We seem to always have one _____ who can negatively impact team spirit.

7. Chris's _____ personality won her many friends.

8. Stan gave a moving, _____ speech.

9. The president _____ his problems by denying any wrong doing.

10. The _____ boy always sat alone in the cafeteria.

RHETORIC
(RET or ik) *n.*
the art or study of using language effectively
and persuasively; over-elaborate language
Link: **RENT-A- WRECK**

CAR SALES

JUST LIKE BRAND NEW,
DRIVES GREAT,
GIRLS WILL LOVE IT.

"A salesman's RENT-A-WRECK RHETORIC."

❑ A person's use of RHETORIC can indicate much about that person's character.

❑ She asked a RHETORICAL question, but he answered anyway.

❑ William Cullen Bryant was a master of RHETORIC and one of our country's most famous editors.

DOGMATIC

(dawg MAT ik) *adj.*

characterized by an authoritative, often
arrogant, assertion of opinions or beliefs

Link: **DOG**

"A DOGMATIC DOG trainer."

- ❑ Grandpa was always DOGMATIC about his views on politics.

- ❑ The tyrant was a DOGMATICAL ruler who would not permit anyone to disagree with him.

- ❑ The opinions or ideas DOGMATICALLY asserted by a DOGMATIC person are knows as DOGMA.

PHILIPPIC

(fe LIP ik) *n.*
a verbal denunciation characterized by
harsh, insulting language; a tirade

Link: **FLIP IT**

*"The cook unleashed a PHILIPPIC when his new
helper couldn't FLIP IT."*

❑ The coach, in seeking to rouse the team,
pronounced bitter **PHILIPPICS** against the
opposing team .

❑ Rachel unleashed a **PHILIPPIC** when her brother
broke her bike.

❑ Dad always directed **PHILIPPICS** at me whenever
I got a bad grade.

PANDEMIC
(pan DEM ik) *adj.*
widespread; general
Link: **PANDA**

"PANDAS are PANDEMIC to China."

- ❏ AIDS has spread in PANDEMIC proportions around the world.

- ❏ Disco's PANDEMIC popularity was short-lived in the 1970's.

- ❏ Boating is a PANDEMIC form of outdoor recreation in Florida.

IDYLLIC
(eye DIL ik) *adj.*
charming in a rustic way: naturally peaceful
Link: **DILL LICK**

"An IDYLLIC DILL LICK."

❑ Chuck and Cathy bought an IDYLLIC cabin in the Smoky Mountains.

❑ Our camping trip was IDYLLIC; we went for long hikes and didn't watch TV all weekend.

❑ Uncle Frank likes to paint IDYLLIC seascapes.

CRYPTIC

(KRIP tik) *adj.*
having an ambiguous or
hidden meaning
Link: **LIPSTICK**

"A CRYPTIC note in LIPSTICK."

☐ Jim's messages were so CRYPTIC; I was baffled by their meaning.

☐ Breaking Germany's CRYPTIC codes during World War II, helped the Allies win the war.

☐ While exploring the cave, we stumbled across a CRYPTIC message written on the wall.

CHOLERIC

(KAHL ur ik) *adj.*
hot-tempered; quick to anger

Link: **COLLAR**

"Our dog became CHOLERIC whenever we COLLARED him."

❑ When my dad gets in one of his CHOLERIC moods, everyone stays clear.

❑ The neighbor's CHOLERIC dog is always chained to the tree.

❑ The bullfighter ran from the CHOLERIC bull.

PECCADILLO
(pek ah DIL oh) *n.*
a slight or trifling sin; a minor offense
Link: ARMADILLO

*"Norm thought running over an
ARMADILLO was a PECCADILLO."*

❑ The reporters were more interested in the
president's personal PECCADILLOES than the
state of the economy.

❑ Being ticketed for running a red light is a mere
PECCADILLO compared to driving while
intoxicated.

❑ Bob couldn't believe he could be punished for the
PECCADILLO of not cleaning his room at
boarding school.

EMPHATIC
(em FAT ik) *adj.*
forcibly expressive
Link: **FAT TICK**

"Rex became EMPHATIC when he saw a FAT TICK on his back."

- ❑ The scientist was EMPHATIC that no materials be brought to the test site.

- ❑ My mom EMPHATICALLY told me to be home by midnight.

- ❑ The sign EMPHATICALLY warned visitors to keep their hands out of the cage.

LOGISTICS

(loh JIS tiks) *n.*

the management of the details of an operation

Link: **LOGS AND STICKS**

*"Lumber mill LOGISTICS consist
of LOGS AND STICKS."*

❏ The Normandy invasion is a great example of military LOGISTICS.

❏ The LOGISTICS involved in building the Golden Gate Bridge required an immense amount of time and resources.

❏ General Eisenhower was an expert of military LOGISTICS.

REVIEW #7: Match the word with its definition.

1. rhetoric – (rent-a-wreck)   a. forcibly expressive
2. dogmatic – (dog)   b. a minor offense
3. philippic – (flip it)   c. over-elaborate language
4. pandemic – (panda)   d. widespread; general
5. idyllic – (dill lick)   e. a verbal denunciation
6. cryptic – (lipstick)   f. quick to anger
7. choleric – (collar)   g. the management of details
8. peccadillo – (armadillo)   h. having a hidden meaning
9. emphatic – (fat tick)   i. naturally peaceful
10. logistics – (logs and sticks) j. an authoritative assertion
                                     of opinions or beliefs

Fill in the blanks with the appropriate word. The word form may need changing.

1. Chuck bought an _____ cabin in the Smoky Mountains.

2. Being ticketed for running a red light is a mere _____ compared to driving while intoxicated.

3. The bullfighter ran from the _____ bull.

4. The Normandy invasion is a great example of military _____.

5. Grandpa was always _____ about his views on politics.

6. My mom _____ told me to be home by midnight.

7. Breaking Germany's _____ codes during World War II, helped the Allies win the war.

8. Rachel unleashed a _____ when her brother broke her bike.

9. She asked a _____ question, but he answered anyway.

10. AIDS has spread in _____ proportions around the world.

CIRCUMSPECT
(SUR kum spekt) *adj.*
cautious; heedful of situations and
potential consequences
Link: **INSPECT**

"A CIRCUMSPECT INSPECTION."

- ❑ In his usual CIRCUMSPECT manner, Frank first assured himself against all losses before making a decision.

- ❑ Pat's five year old CIRCUMSPECTLY looks both ways before crossing the street.

- ❑ Because the judge was CIRCUMSPECT, he was usually considered impartial.

ABSTRACT

(AB strakt) *adj.*
difficult to understand;
impersonal; theoretical
Link: CONTRACT

*"Be wary of salesmen with
ABSTRACT CONTRACTS."*

- ❑ Though Joshua thought his ideas were sound, we considered them ABSTRACT.

- ❑ Dad's paintings were ABSTRACTIONS, we couldn't tell what they were.

- ❑ Christopher's directions to his house were so ABSTRACT we were lost for two hours.

DEFUNCT

(dee FUNGKT) *adj.*
dead or inactive; having
ceased to exist

Link: **JUNK**

"Chinese JUNKS are now DEFUNCT."

- ❑ Latin is a DEFUNCT language.

- ❑ Although Shakespeare has been dead for centuries, his plays will never be DEFUNCT.

- ❑ In <u>Moby Dick</u>, Ishmael tells the story of a DEFUNCT whaling ship, the <u>Pequod</u>.

SUCCINCT

(sek SINGKT) *adj.*
brief and to the point;
concise and terse

Link: **SINK**

*"Virginia was SUCCINCT when Ernie
forgot to fix the SINK."*

- ❑ When Joe was called upon, he SUCCINCTLY paraphrased what the teacher had just explained.

- ❑ Benjamin Franklin's aphorisms are so SUCCINCT that they are still used today.

- ❑ The mother's reprimand was SUCCINCT but effective.

PALPABLE
(PAL pah bul) *adj.*
capable of being touched or felt
Link: PAL THE BULL

"Our PAL, THE BULL, is PALPABLE."

❑ The PALPABLE imagery helps make the poem more realistic.

❑ The answer is as PALPABLE as the nose on your face.

❑ Fear ran PALPABLY through the crowd as the man wielded a pistol.

ACCOUNTABLE
(ah KOWNT uh bul) *adj.*
expected to answer for one's actions;
responsible, liable, answerable
Link: **COUNT THE BULLS**

*"Don, the accountant, was ACCOUNTABLE for
COUNTING THE BULLS."*

❑ Timothy was ACCOUNTABLE for counting the votes after the election.

❑ Laura said she was not ACCOUNTABLE for the problems her sister had created.

❑ You can't hold the cat ACCOUNTABLE for the mess it made because the dog chased it through the kitchen.

OSTENSIBLE
(o STEN seh bul) *adj.*
appearing as such; offered as
genuine or real
Link: **SENSIBLE**

*"Taking the short-cut was OSTENSIBLY not the
SENSIBLE thing to do."*

☐ OSTENSIBLY the purpose of the assignment is to
teach students to do research.

☐ The OSTENSIBLE reason that Mr. Jones became
a substitute teacher was because he needed the
money.

☐ The OSTENSIBLE purpose of this book is to
improve the reader's vocabulary.

PLIABLE
(PLYE ah bul) *adj.*
receptive to change; easily persuaded or
controlled; easily bent or twisted
Link: **FLY BULL**

"A PLIABLE BULL convinced he can FLY."

❑ Students demonstrate their PLIABILITY when they remain open to new ideas.

❑ Putty is a PLIABLE material that can be easily shaped.

❑ Bob was always PLIABLE to Brenda's demands.

ADROIT

(ah DROIT) *adj.*
skillful; deft

Link: **DETROIT**

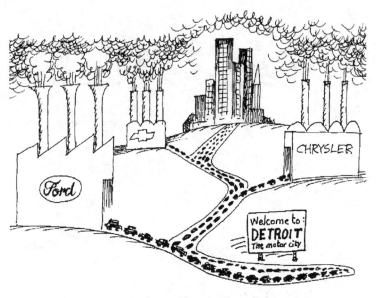

*"The auto workers of DETROIT are ADROIT at
manufacturing automobiles."*

❑ Many fourth graders are more ADROIT on the
computer than their parents.

❑ Mr. Smith ADROITLY removed Eric from the
class before he could cause a problem.

❑ Sebastian always wins at cards because he is so
ADROIT at counting the cards that have been
played.

BAUBLE
(BAW bul) *n.*
a small, inexpensive trinket
Link: **BULL**

"A BULL'S BAUBLE."

❑ Never one for BAUBLES, Diane always wore real diamonds.

❑ Mixed among the precious gems in Jennifer's jewelry box were costume jewelry and other BAUBLES.

❑ The child was delighted with the BAUBLE she received from her aunt.

REVIEW #8: Match the word with its definition.

1. circumspect – (inspect)
2. abstract – (contract)
3. defunct – (junk)
4. succinct – (sink)
5. palpable – (pal the bull)
6. accountable – (count the bulls)
7. ostensible- (sensible)
8. pliable – (fly bull)
9. adroit – (Detroit)
10. bauble – (bull)

a. brief and to the point
b. responsible
c. skillful; deft
d. difficult to understand
e. a small trinket
f. dead or inactive
g. easily persuaded
h. cautious
i. appearing as such
j. capable of being touched

Fill in the blanks with the appropriate word. The word form may need changing.

1. The _____ reason that Mr. Jones became a substitute teacher was because he needed the money.

2. The mother's reprimand was _____ but effective.

3. Bob was always _____ to Brenda's demands.

4. Christopher's directions to his house were so _____ we were lost for two hours.

5. Timothy was _____ for counting the votes after the election.

6. Many fourth graders are more _____ than their parents.

7. Although Shakespeare has been dead for centuries, his plays will never be _____.

8. Never one for _____, Diane always wore real diamonds.

9. The _____ imagery helps make the poem more realistic.

10. Little Billy _____ looked both ways before crossing the street.

SKULLDUGGERY
(skul DUG uh ree) *n.*
trickery; underhandedness
Link: **SKULL DUG**

"Young Indiana Jones was up to some SKULLDUGGERY."

❑ The charlatan was guilty of SKULLDUGGERY.

❑ In order to capture ships at sea, pirates would practice all types of SKULLDUGGERY to gain an advantage over their prey.

❑ After his arrest, he admitted to numerous counts of SKULLDUGGERY that had plagued his town for years.

ANCILLARY

(AN sih ler ee) *adj.*
helping; providing assistance;
subordinate

Link: **CELERY**

"The CELERY was ANCILLARY to Peter's sandwich."

❑ Christopher worked hard to earn an ANCILLARY income.

❑ Our chemistry workbook is ANCILLARY to the textbook.

❑ The queen has her ANCILLARY maid prepare her clothes each morning.

SEDENTARY

(SED en ter ee) *adj.*
characterized by or requiring much sitting;
accustomed to little exercise

Link: SIT AND STARE

"SEDENTARY Larry often would SIT AND STARE."

- ❑ "A SEDENTARY lifestyle can lead to heart problems," the doctor explained as he urged the patient to exercise regularly.

- ❑ Because of a stroke, the normally active woman was forced to lead a more SEDENTARY life.

- ❑ The SEDENTARY nature of a secretary's job would make it impractical for a restless person.

CURSORY

(KUR suh ree) *adj.*

rapid and superficial; performed with haste
and scant attention to detail

Link: CURSE

*"A CURSORY glance by the prince told him
Cinderella's foot had been CURSED."*

- ❏ Dad's CURSORY effort to repair the roof made it leak even more.

- ❏ The general berated the private for his CURSORY attempt to clean his locker.

- ❏ The general contractor was so CURSORY in the construction of our home that he forgot to lay the plumbing lines.

PREDATORY

(PRED ah tor ee) *adj.*
victimizing or destroying others
for one's own gain; pillaging
Link: **BREAD STORY**

"A PREDATORY BREAD STORY."

- ❑ The tiger shark not only looks PREDATORY, but is a PREDATOR.

- ❑ The killer whale is a PREDATORY mammal that is rarely known to harm humans.

- ❑ During the Middle Ages, many PREDATORY bands of men roamed England.

SYMMETRY

(SIM i tree) *n.*
exact correspondence of form on
opposite sides of a dividing line
Link: CEMETERY

"SYMMETRY in the CEMETERY."

- ❏ The SYMMETRY of the garden added to its beauty.

- ❏ The Tower Bridge has a SYMMETRY unequaled in London's architecture.

- ❏ The SYMMETRY of a rose is so perfect and so simple, yet man cannot duplicate it.

TAWDRY
(TAW dree) *adj.*
gaudy and cheap in appearance
or nature
Link: **AUDREY**

"TAWDRY AUDREY."

❑ Scott gave Rhonda a TAWDRY engagement ring and could tell by her face that she didn't like it.

❑ Shirley's TAWDRY dress was the talk of all the gossips.

❑ The innocent children believed the TAWDRY jewels in their mother's bureau were worth a fortune.

AMBULATORY
(AM byu lah tor ee) *adj.*
of or for walking; capable of walking
Link: AMBULANCE

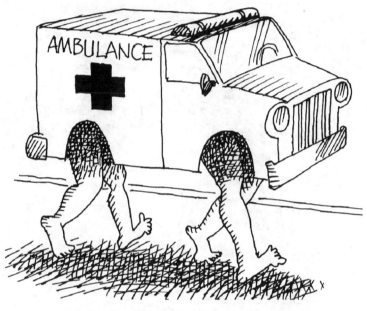

"An AMBULATORY AMBULANCE."

❑ Although Robin's foot was in a cast, she was still AMBULATORY.

❑ Most AMBULATORY patients do not stay overnight at the hospital.

❑ The ninety eight year old woman was not simply AMBULATORY; she was spry.

IDOLATRY

(I doll ah tree) *n.*
blind or excessive devotion to something

Link: **DOLL TREE**

*"The twins' love of their DOLL TREE
bordered on IDOLATRY."*

- ❑ Ben's parents worried about his IDOLATRY to the occult.

- ❑ Elvis' IDOLATROUS fans stormed Graceland.

- ❑ Peter has an IDOLATROUS addiction for the game of golf.

PECUNIARY

(pi KYOO nee er ee) *adj.*

consisting of or relating to money

Link: **PECULIAR DAIRY**

"A PECUNIARY PECULIAR DAIRY."

☐ Alex's concerns about college were specifically PECUNIARY.

☐ Ryan wanted to take Jessie to the prom but didn't ask her because of his PECUNIARY problems.

☐ PECUNIARY troubles are the primary reason for many failed marriages.

REVIEW #9: **Match the word with its definition.**

1. skullduggery – (skull dug)
2. ancillary – (celery)
3. sedentary – (sit and stare)
4. cursory – (curse)
5. predatory – (bread story)
6. symmetry – (cemetery)
7. tawdry – (Audrey)
8. ambulatory – (ambulance)
9. idolatry – (doll tree)
10. pecuniary – (peculiar dairy)

a. subordinate; helping
b. gaudy and cheap
c. victimizing; pillaging
d. exact correspondence
e. accustomed to little exercise
f. trickery
g. excessive devotion
h. relating to money
i. capable of walking
j. performed with haste

Fill in the blanks with the appropriate word. The word form may need changing.

1. Although Robin's foot was still in a cast, she was still _____.

2. Dad's _____ effort to repair the roof made it leak even more.

3. The _____ of the garden added to its beauty.

4. Ben's parents worried about his _____ to the occult.

5. Our chemistry workbook is _____ to the textbook.

6. Because of a stroke, the normally active woman was forced to lead a more _____ life.

7. Alex's concerns about college were specifically _____.

8. During the Middle Ages, many _____ bands of men roamed England.

9. In order to capture ships at sea, pirates would practice all types of _____ to gain an advantage over their prey.

10. Shirley's _____ dress was the talk of all the gossips.

113

PANORAMA

(pan ah RAM ah) *n.*

an unbroken view of a wide area

Link: CAMERA

"A PANORAMIC CAMERA."

❑ We enjoyed the scenic PANORAMA while taking a hot air balloon ride.

❑ The PANORAMIC view from the top of the Empire State Building is spectacular.

❑ The Grand Canyon offers PANORAMIC views of great splendor.

SAGA

(SAH gah) *n.*
a long story, often telling the
history of a family

Link: GAGA

"A GAGA SAGA."

- ❑ The SAGA of Odysseus has been retold throughout history.

- ❑ I thought Jennifer wanted to tell me about her argument with her mother, but after twenty minutes I could see it was turning into a SAGA.

- ❑ Moby Dick is a SAGA of the sea written by Herman Melville.

PLETHORA
(PLETH or ah) *n.*
a state of excessive fullness; superabundance
Link: **FLORA**

"A PLETHORA of FLORA."

- ❏ There was an awesome PLETHORA of food at the picnic.

- ❏ Jake opened the back door and a PLETHORA of mosquitoes flew in.

- ❏ After placing an ad in the paper to sell my Corvette for $200, I received a PLETHORA of calls.

GRADIENT

(GRAY dee unt) *n.*
a rate of inclination; a slope

Link: **GREAT AUNT**

*"It's tough getting a GREAT AUNT
up a steep GRADIENT."*

❑ The GRADIENT of the hill made it difficult to peddle my bike.

❑ The GRADIENT of metabolism is important in the field of biology.

❑ The teacher put the grades on a GRADIENT so that more students would do well on the hard test.

ADHERENT

(ad HEER unt) *n.*

a follower of a leader; supporter

Link: ADHERE

"An ADHERENT ADHERING to his leader."

- ❏ The political candidate praised his ADHERENTS for their support.

- ❏ People who believe in a particular religion are said to be ADHERENTS of that faith.

- ❏ Though the divorced princess was no longer part of the royal family, she continued to claim many ADHERENTS.

VENT
(vent) *n.*
a means of escape or release;
an outlet; a small hole
Link: VENT

"Professor Jones VENTING his frustration."

❑ George felt the need to VENT his anger in class even if it resulted in suspension.

❑ As the boys searched the coastline, they found a VENT in which they could hide.

❑ At the funeral everyone gave VENT to their emotions by openly weeping.

ARMAMENT
(ARM ah ment) *n.*
military supplies and weapons; the
process of arming for war
Link: ARM

"The long ARMS of ARMAMENT."

❑ The United States government believes its nuclear
ARMAMENT is a deterrent to the possibility of a
third world war.

❑ We equipped ourselves with a an ARMAMENT
no enemy could match.

❑ Christopher is the ARMAMENTS officer for his
division.

PRESENTIMENT
(pre ZEN tih ment) *n.*
a sense that something is about to
occur; a premonition
Link: **PRESENT**

*"Ted had a PRESENTIMENT that he was not going
to like his PRESENT."*

❏ Ray had a PRESENTIMENT that he would hear
from Tony before the end of the day.

❏ Jane's PRESENTIMENT was that one of us
would win an Oscar at the Academy Awards.

❏ The sage had a PRESENTIMENTAL vision of an
impending disaster that would befall the village.

CORPULENT

(KOR pew lent) *n.*
fat; obese
Link: **CORPORAL**

"A CORPULENT CORPORAL."

- England's King Henry VIII was known for his CORPULENT build.

- Some football players look CORPULENT but are actually very muscular.

- CORPULENT is a euphemism for fat.

CIRCUMVENT

(sur kum VENT) *v.*
to surround; enclose; bypass

Link: CIRCLE TENT

"The Indians CIRCUMVENTED the TENT."

☐ We were able to CIRCUMVENT the heavy traffic by taking a short-cut.

☐ The politician CIRCUMVENTED an argument by changing the subject.

☐ The general CIRCUMVENTED the enemy by distracting them with a minor campaign.

REVIEW #10: Match the word with its definition.

1. panorama – (camera)
2. saga – (gaga)
3. plethora – (flora)
4. gradient – (great aunt)
5. adherent – (adhere)
6. vent – (vent)
7. armament – (arm)
8. presentiment – (present)
9. corpulent – (corporal)
10. circumvent – (circle tent)

a. military supplies
b. a wide view of an area
c. supporter
d. a means of escape
e. fat; obese
f. a slope
g. a long story
h. to surround; bypass
i. superabundance
j. a sense that something is about to occur

Fill in the blanks with the appropriate word. The word form may need changing.

1. The _____ of the hill made it difficult to peddle my bike.

2. The United States government believes its nuclear _____ is a deterrent to the possibility of a third world war.

3. The _____ of Odysseus has been retold throughout history.

4. We were able to _____ the heavy traffic by taking a short-cut.

5. We enjoyed the scenic _____ while taking a hot air balloon ride.

6. George felt the need to _____ his anger in class even if it resulted in suspension.

7. Ray had a _____ that he would hear from Tony before the end of the day.

8. The political candidate praised his _____ for their support.

9. There was an awesome _____ of food at the picnic.

10. King Henry VIII was known for his _____ build.

ATONE
(ah TONE) *v.*
to make amends
Link: **ALONE**

"He who does not ATONE, ends up ALONE."

- ❏ Rachel ATONED for skipping school by getting straight A's on her next report card.

- ❏ Nothing the convicted murderer said could ATONE for his crime.

- ❏ After ATONING for his past indiscretions, the President quickly won back the support of the nation.

DEVOID

(di VOID) *adj.*
entirely without; lacking
Link: **AVOID**

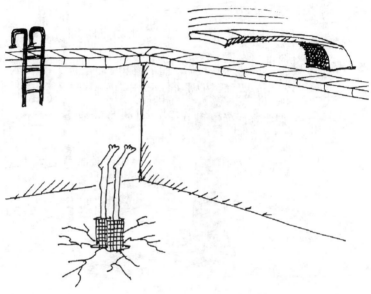

"AVOID diving into a pool DEVOID of water."

- ❑ It was apparent that Bill was DEVOID of table manners as we watched him eat his entire meal with his fingers.

- ❑ The island was DEVOID of drinking water.

- ❑ Our football team is totally DEVOID of an offense; we haven't scored a touchdown in the last four games.

REPLETE
(ri PLEET) *adj.*
full or supplied to the utmost;
gorge
Link: **PETE**

*"PETE was REPLETE with supplies
for his camping trip."*

- ❏ We ordered our pizza with "the works"; it was REPLETE with sausage, ham, pepperoni, olives, onions, and anchovies.

- ❏ The students love the novel because it is REPLETE with adventures.

- ❏ The buffet was REPLETE with many tantalizing dishes.

MAMMOTH
(MAM uth) *adj.*
huge; gigantic
Link: MOTH

"A MAMMOTH MOTH."

- ❑ Until I visited Manhattan, I could not imagine the MAMMOTH size of the Empire State Building.

- ❑ Herman Melville's title character, Moby Dick, is a MAMMOTH whale.

- ❑ When Jane returned from vacation, she found a MAMMOTH amount of work piled on her desk.

BALEFUL
(BAYL ful) *adj.*
threatening; hurtful; malignant;
ominous
Link: **BALE FALL**

"A BALEFUL BALE FALLING."

❑ The prisoner sat in BALEFUL silence while the judge read his jail sentence.

❑ Gertrude cast a BALEFUL glance at her boyfriend when he said she had gained a lot of weight.

❑ The sky was BALEFULLY thick with clouds.

DIMINUTION

(di muh NYOO shun) *n.*
the act or process of diminishing;
reduction

Link: **AMMUNITION**

"A DIMINUTION of AMMUNITION."

- ❑ The crew of the crippled research submarine were concerned with the DIMINUTION of their air supply.

- ❑ There was an obvious DIMINUTION of the temperature as the sun began to set.

- ❑ Due to the higher cost of living, Drew noticed a DIMINUTION of his checking account.

PURBLIND
(per blind) *adj.*
having poor vision; nearly or
partly blind
Link: **PURR BLIND**

"The PURBLIND cat PURRED as it was led by its seeing-eye mouse."

- ❑ I am afraid that when it comes to mathematics, I am PURBLIND.

- ❑ The PURBLIND man was undergoing surgery to restore his sight.

- ❑ One of the most famous of PURBLIND people, who was able to overcome her handicap, was Helen Keller.

ETHEREAL
(i THEER ee ul) *adj.*
very light; airy; delicate; heavenly
Link: **CEREAL**

"ETHEREAL CEREAL."

❑ An ETHEREAL mist covered the hill in the morning.

❑ The ETHEREAL scent of freshly baked apple pie permeated the kitchen.

❑ Elizabeth had the singing voice of an ETHEREAL angel.

LACKADAISICAL
(lak ah DAY zi kul) *adj.*
showing lack of interest; listless
Link: **YAK IN THE DAISIES**

"A LACKADAISICAL YAK IN THE DAISIES."

- ❑ Margaret's LACKADAISICAL attitude will hurt her chances of getting into college.

- ❑ He just stood there LACKADAISICALLY staring into space.

- ❑ I would not want to go to a doctor who had a LACKADAISICAL approach to his practice.

BLAND
(bland) *adj.*
lacking flavor or zest; dull
Link: LAND

*"After months at sea Columbus kissed
the LAND, but found it BLAND."*

☐ The pudding was smooth though BLAND.

☐ The doctor put Edgar on a BLAND diet to soothe
his stomach problems.

☐ Christopher's BLAND sense of humor was often
misunderstood.

REVIEW #11: Match the word with its definition.

1. atone – (alone)
2. replete – (Pete)
3. mammoth – (moth)
4. baleful – (bail fall)
5. diminution – (ammunition)
6. purblind – (purr blind)
7. ethereal – (cereal)
8. lackadaisical – (yak in the daisies)
9. bland – (land)
10. devoid – (avoid)

a. threatening; ominous
b. lacking flavor
c. to make amends
d. entirely without
e. showing lack of interest
f. huge; gigantic
g. reduction
h. full
i. having poor vision
j. very light; heavenly

Fill in the blanks with the appropriate word. The word form may need changing.

1. Until I visited Manhattan, I could not imagine the _____ size of the Empire State Building.

2. Gertrude cast a _____ glance at her boyfriend when he said she had gained a lot of weight.

3. An _____ mist covered the hill in the morning.

4. He just stood there _____ staring into space.

5. We ordered our pizza with "the works"; it was _____ with sausage, ham, pepperoni, olives, onions, and anchovies.

6. The island was _____ of drinking water.

7. Nothing the convicted murderer said could _____ for his crime.

8. There was an obvious _____ of the temperature as the sun began to set.

9. The doctor put Edgar on a _____ diet to soothe his stomach problems.

10. The _____ man was undergoing surgery to restore his sight.

CASCADE

(kas KAYD) *n.*
a waterfall; anything resembling
a waterfall
Link: **LEMONADE**

"A CASCADE of LEMONADE."

❑ Rachel's hair formed a beautiful CASCADE down her back.

❑ A cloud of confetti CASCADED down onto the crowd celebrating the New Year.

❑ When Marta hit the jackpot, coins CASCADED from the slot machine.

PALISADE
(pal ih SAYD) *n.*
a fortification of timbers set in the
ground; an extended cliff
Link: **PAL IN THE SHADE**

*"My PAL IN THE SHADE prefers to sit
under the PALISADES."*

- ❑ The king built a PALISADE to fortify his castle.

- ❑ The PALISADES of the Grand Canyon are a natural beauty one must visit to appreciate.

- ❑ The PALISADE followed the course of the river, winding its way through the canyon.

FUSILLADE
(FYOO se lahd) *n.*
a rapid outburst or barrage
Link: **FUSELAGE**

*"The aircraft FUSELAGE received a
FUSILLADE of gunfire."*

- ❑ Sally ran to her window after the FUSILLADE of stones awakened her.

- ❑ The guard of the moat was surprised by a FUSILLADE of arrows which allowed the invaders to gain entrance to the castle.

- ❑ After her flawless skating performance, Andrea received a FUSILLADE of bouquets.

PARABLE
(PAR ah bul) *n.*
a simple story illustrating a moral or religious lesson
Link: **PAIR OF BULLS**

"A PAIR OF BULLS reading a PARABLE."

❑ My son's favorite book is one full of PARABLES.

❑ The story of the boy who cried wolf is a PARABLE about the consequences of telling lies.

❑ John's favorite part of Sunday school is when the teacher reads a PARABLE.

PARADIGM
(PAR ah dime) *n.*
a pattern that serves as a model or example
Link: **PAIR OF DIMES**

*"A PARADIGM of the new
PAIR OF DIMES."*

- ❏ Michael Jordan is a PARADIGM of a professional basketball player.

- ❏ When designing the Luxor Hotel in Las Vegas the architects used the Great Pyramids of Egypt as their PARADIGM.

- ❏ The Model-T was used as a PARADIGM by many automobile manufacturers in the early 1900's.

PATRIARCH
(PAY tree ahrk) *n.*
the leader of a family or tribe
Link: **PASTRY ART**

"The PATRIARCH'S specialty is PASTRY ART."

❑ Abraham is considered one of the PATRIARCHS of the Hebrew religion.

❑ William Bradford led the pilgrims to the new world and acted as PATRIARCH of the colony.

❑ The PATRIARCH is the one the tribe turns to for leadership and guidance.

MALADROIT

(mal uh DROYT) *adj.*

clumsy; inept

Link: **DRAW IT**

"The MALADROIT artist couldn't DRAW IT."

- ❑ The MALADROIT painter spilled a can of paint on our new carpet.

- ❑ Actor, Charlie Chaplin, was famous for his MALADROIT roles.

- ❑ Bob was upset with the mechanic's MALADROIT attempt to repair his car.

MALAISE
(ma LAYZ) *n.*
a vague feeling of bodily discomfort,
as at the beginning of an illness
Link: **MAYONNAISE**

"Hal's MALAISE was brought on by spoiled MAYONNAISE."

- ❏ Samantha's MALAISE was later diagnosed as food poisoning.

- ❏ Beth's MALAISE began when she awoke with a sore throat.

- ❏ A sudden MALAISE overcame Jonathan when the postman delivered a certified letter from the IRS.

MALICE

(MAL is) *n.*
a desire or intention to harm
others or see them suffer
Link: **ALICE**

*"ALICE has MALICE towards door
to door salesmen."*

- ☐ The prisoner was not granted parole because his MALICE was still obvious.

- ☐ Our government is based on justice, with MALICE toward none.

- ☐ We could not believe that such a young girl could harbor such MALICE toward her neighbors.

MALODOR
(mal OH dor) *n.*
a bad odor
Link: **BAD ODOR**

"Barnyard MALODOR."

- ❑ After the storm, the MALODOR made it clear that the sewers were not working.

- ❑ A MALODOROUS stench filled the car after we ran over the skunk.

- ❑ The MALODOR of the stray dog kept us at arm's length.

145

REVIEW #12: **Match the word with its definition.**

1. cascade – (lemonade)
2. palisade – (pal in the shade)
3. fusillade – (fuselage)
4. parable – (pair of bulls)
5. paradigm – (pair of dimes)
6. patriarch – (pastry art)
7. maladroit – (draw it)
8. malaise – (mayonnaise)
9. malice – (Alice)
10. malodor – (bad odor)

a. clumsy; inept
b. a simple story
c. a leader
d. a rapid outburst
e. a desire to harm others
f. a bad odor
g. a model
h. a feeling of becoming ill
i. resembling a waterfall
j. a fortification of timbers

Fill in the blanks with the appropriate word. The word form may need changing.

1. William Bradford led the pilgrims to the new world and acted as _____ of the colony.

2. The king built a _____ to fortify his castle.

3. The _____ painter spilled a can of paint on our new carpet.

4. The guard of the moat was surprised by a _____ of arrows which allowed the invaders to gain entrance to the castle.

5. Rachel's hair formed a beautiful _____ down her back.

6. The prisoner was not granted parole because his _____ was still obvious.

7. The story of the boy who cried wolf is a _____ about the consequences of telling lies.

8. After the storm, the _____ made it clear that the sewers were not working.

9. Samantha's _____ was later diagnosed as food poisoning.

10. The Model-T was used as a _____ by many automobile manufactures in the early 1990's.

PARAGON
(PAR ah gon) *n.*
a model or pattern of excellence
Link: **PAIR OF GUNS**

"A PARAGON PAIR OF GUNS."

❑ Although Joyce was a PARAGON of virtue, she was also good fun to be with at the same time.

❑ While not an architectural PARAGON to be copied, the sturdy old brick house has withstood many hurricanes.

❑ William named his shoe company PARAGON Shoes, with expectations customers would think his shoes the best.

STRIFE
(stryfe) *n.*
bitter conflict; quarrel; fight
Link: **LIFE**

"There was little STRIFE in Amanda's LIFE."

- ❏ He was thin and gaunt and had led a life full of STRIFE.

- ❏ It was a time of great STRIFE in the kingdom because of three seasons of failed crops.

- ❏ A life of poverty is filled with much STRIFE.

APPEASE
(ah PEEZ) *v.*
to soothe; to pacify or relieve by
giving into
Link: **PEAS**

"To APPEASE his parents, Johnny ate his PEAS."

- ❏ To APPEASE his mother, Zachary always walked the dog before dinner.

- ❏ The sergeant APPEASED his troops by giving them an extra day of rest and relaxation.

- ❏ The trainer APPEASES the monkey by giving him extra bananas.

LAMPOON
(lam POON) *n.*
a light, good-humored satire
Link: HARPOON

A LAMPOON with a HARPOON.

- ❑ In a humorous skit, the comedian LAMPOONED the president.

- ❑ When the boss leaves the office, Sylvester always LAMPOONS the poor man's lisp.

- ❑ <u>MAD</u> magazine LAMPOONS many aspects of American culture.

BOON
(boon) *n.*
a timely benefit; a blessing
Link: **BABOON**

"A BOON for BABOONS."

- ❑ Construction of the new residential development was a BOON to the community.

- ❑ The week-long rain was a BOON to the farmers whose crops were withering from the drought.

- ❑ The decline of interest rates proved a BOON to the real estate market; more families could afford to buy homes.

POLTROON
(pol TROON) *n.*
a coward
Link: **PLATOON**

"A PLATOON full of POLTROONS."

- ❑ Although Joe did not want the guys to think he was a POLTROON, he knew what they wanted him to do was dangerous.

- ❑ He was found guilty of POLTROONERY for deserting his men while they were under attack.

- ❑ Many considered him a POLTROON because he was in his 30's yet still afraid of the dark.

BRAZEN
(BRAY zun) *adj.*
bold, shameless; impudent;
also like brass
Link: **RAISIN**

"A BRAZEN RAISIN."

- ❑ Robert's BRAZEN presumption that he would be elected class president because of his good looks proved wrong when the votes were counted.

- ❑ Tiger Woods' BRAZEN attempt to reach the green in two strokes paid off with a birdie.

- ❑ The BRAZENNESS of the cymbals worn by the dancers made metallic, melodious sounds.

CONUNDRUM

(kuh NUN drum) *n.*
a dilemma; any problem or puzzle
Link: **NUN'S DRUM**

"The NUN'S DRUMS created a CONUNDRUM."

❑ In most mystery novels, the CONUNDRUM is solved by the end.

❑ Justin's CONUNDRUM after high school was whether he should go find a job or go to college first.

❑ During the long drive, Jean invented entertaining CONUNDRUMS to help keep Jeff awake.

COVERT
(KOH vert) *adj.*
secret; hidden; concealed
Link: **COVER**

*"Secret agents act COVERTLY to
COVER their true identities."*

❑ Sam carried out COVERT missions for the CIA in
China during the Korean War.

❑ Spies usually operate COVERTLY.

❑ OVERT is the opposite of COVERT. OVERT
means open or unconcealed.

BOOTLEG

(BOOT leg) *v.*
to smuggle; to make, sell, or
transport for sale illegally

Link: **BOOTS AND LEGS**

*"Stan was caught with BOOTLEG
BOOTS AND LEGS."*

❑ Scott was arrested when he attempted to sell a
BOOTLEG CD.

❑ During Prohibition, all liquor in the United States
was BOOTLEG.

❑ On the streets of some cities BOOTLEGGERS sell
just about anything.

REVIEW #13: Match the word with its definition.

1. paragon – (pair of guns)
2. strife – (life)
3. appease – (peas)
4. lampoon – (harpoon)
5. boon – (baboon)
6. poltroon – (platoon)
7. brazen – (raisin)
8. conundrum – (nun's drum)
9. covert – (cover)
10. bootleg – (boots and legs)

a. a coward
b. secret; hidden
c. bitter conflict; fight
d. a dilemma
e. a model of excellence
f. a light good-humored satire
g. bold; shameless
h. to soothe or pacify
i. to smuggle; sell illegally
j. a timely benefit

Fill in the blanks with the appropriate word. The word form may need changing.

1. Sam carried out _____ missions for the CIA in China during the Korean War.

2. To _____ his mother, Zackary always walked the dog before dinner.

3. In a humorous skit, the comedian _____ the president.

4. He was thin and gaunt and had led a life full of _____.

5. Scott was arrested when he attempted to sell a _____ CD.

6. Construction of the new residential development was a _____ to the community.

7. Tiger Woods' _____ attempt to reach the green in two strokes paid off with a birdie.

8. Many considered him a _____ because he was in his 30's yet still afraid of the dark.

9. Justin's _____ after high school was whether he should get a job or go to college.

10. Although Joyce was a _____ of virtue, she was good fun to be with at the same time.

DIATRIBE

(DYE uh tryb) *n.*

a bitter verbal attack

Link: **TRIBE**

"Sitting Bull retaliated with a DIATRIBE after his TRIBE was pied in the face."

❑ Coach Johnson's DIATRIBE was futile because the referee refused to reverse his decision.

❑ The prosecuting attorney began his opening statement with a DIATRIBE directed toward the defendant.

❑ After being struck by a water balloon, the old man retaliated with a lengthy DIATRIBE which scared away the deviant kids.

OFFAL

(AW fal) *n.*
waste parts especially of a
butchered animal; rubbish

Link: **AWFUL**

"The OFFAL smelled AWFUL."

- ❑ The dog rooted through the OFFAL for scraps of food.

- ❑ The young cheetah left the OFFAL of his prey to the buzzards.

- ❑ The butcher saved the OFFAL for his dogs.

PARLEY
(PAHR lee) *n.*
a conference, especially between enemies
Link: **PARTY**

"The PARLEY turned into a PARTY."

❏ A PARLEY was scheduled between the leaders of the opposing nations.

❏ The National Football League owners and players PARLEYED to reach a settlement of salary caps.

❏ After a brief PARLEY, the defense attorney and prosecuting attorney agreed to settle the dispute out of court.

FRAY

(fray) *n.*
fight or scuffle; brawl
Link: **HAY**

"A FRAY in the HAY."

- ❑ The party turned into a FRAY when the bikers showed up.

- ❑ A FRAY occurred in the cafeteria when Kirk spilled his lunch on Jody.

- ❑ When Mark was beaned by the pitcher, a FRAY ensued between the teams.

LAMBASTE

(lam BAST) *v.*

to give a thrashing; scold

Link: **LAMB**

*"The LAMB took a LAMBASTING
from the champ."*

- ❑ The drill sergeant LAMBASTED his troops for their poor performance on the obstacle course.

- ❑ George received a verbal LAMBASTING from his father for not doing his chores.

- ❑ The fierce storm LAMBASTED the ship and its crew.

CATACLYSM

(KAT ah kliz um) *n.*
a violent upheaval or change

Link: CAT CLINTON

*"President CLINTON'S CAT is about
to create a CATACLYSM."*

☐ The CATACLYSM generated by World War I had effects which lasted for generations.

☐ The sudden earthquake was CATACLYSMIC in its destruction.

☐ The United Nations does everything within its power to avoid the CATACLYSM of a third World War.

ESCAPADE

(ES kah payd) *n.*

an adventurous unconventional act

Link: **ICE CAPADES**

"An ESCAPADE at the ICE CAPADES."

- ❑ Mary's ESCAPADE was harmless, but it caused her parents some concern.

- ❑ Joe and Alan's ESCAPADE at the beach during Spring Break is one they will never forget.

- ❑ Hiking in the Rockies was our most recent family ESCAPADE.

ESCHEW
(ES choo) *v.*
to avoid or shun
Link: **AH CHEW**

"It is a good policy to ESCHEW all AH CHEWS!"

❏ We were advised to ESCHEW riding the subway at night.

❏ The doctor told Danny to ESCHEW the sun's dangerous rays by applying sunscreen whenever he went outside.

❏ Sally ESCHEWS anyone who uses bad language.

RANSACK

(RAN sak) *v.*

to search thoroughly; pillage

Link: **RAN SACK**

*"The police RAN in SACKS to RANSACK
the suspect's apartment."*

❏ April had to RANSACK her room in order to find the overdue library book.

❏ The thieves not only broke in, but they also RANSACKED the office looking for valuables.

❏ The king and his men were busy RANSACKING the village and did not know a truce had been called.

CAMARADERIE
(kah mah RAH der ee) *n.*
comradeship; friendship
Link: **COMRADES THREE**

"CAMARADERIE amongst THREE COMRADES."

- ❑ The girls developed such a CAMARADERIE in college that they remained friends for life.

- ❑ People find their jobs more enjoyable if there is a sense of CAMARADERIE in their work place.

- ❑ Because we are both Miami Dolphins fans, we had an instant CAMARADERIE.

167

REVIEW #14: Match the word with its definition.

1. diatribe – (tribe)
2. offal – (awful)
3. parley – (party)
4. fray – (hay)
5. lambaste – (lamb)
6. cataclysm – (cat Clinton)
7. escapade – (ice capades)
8. eschew – (ah chew)
9. ransack – (ran sack)
10. camaraderie – (comrades three)

a. to avoid
b. a brawl or fight
c. to search thoroughly
d. an adventurous act
e. waste parts
f. to give a thrashing
g. a conference between enemies
h. a violent upheaval
i. a verbal attack
j. friendship

Fill in the blanks with the appropriate word. The word form may need changing.

1. We were told to _____ riding the subway at night.

2. The coach's _____ directed at the referee was futile.

3. The fierce storm _____ the ship and its crew.

4. A _____ was scheduled between the leaders of the opposing nations.

5. April had to _____ her room in order to find the overdue library book.

6. Because we are both Miami Dolphin fans, we had an instant _____.

7. The butcher saved the _____ for his dogs.

8. Hiking in the Rockies was our most recent family _____.

9. The _____ generated by World War I had effects which lasted for generations.

10. A _____ occurred in the cafeteria when Kirk spilled his lunch on Jody.

ICONOCLAST

(I con o klast) *n.*
one who attacks and seeks to overthrow traditional
or popular ideas or institutions

Link: **KIND TO THE PAST**

"An ICONOCLAST not KIND TO THE PAST."

❑ Troy's ICONOCLASTIC views were not popular with his parents.

❑ Young voters were attracted to the candidate's ICONOCLASTIC platform.

❑ Thomas Edison was a great ICONOCLAST; without his ICONOCLASTIC views we might still be sitting in the dark.

SAGE
(sayj) *n.*
a person of wisdom and prudence
Link: **PAGE**

"The SAGE reads each PAGE."

- ❑ During ancient times a SAGE was consulted for momentous decisions.

- ❑ Native American tribes regarded their medicine man as a SAGE with special healing powers.

- ❑ In our family we consider our grandparents the SAGES of the family.

NEMESIS

(NEM eh sis) *n.*

an opponent that cannot be beaten or overcome

Link: **MY SIS**

"My NEMESIS is MY SIS."

❏ Lex Luther considers Superman his NEMESIS.

❏ Tom is my NEMESIS because I can beat everyone who beats him in tennis, but I can't beat him.

❏ Potato chips are Paul's NEMESIS; if he takes one bite he can't stop eating them.

DOLT

(DOHLT) *n.*
a stupid person
Link: **VOLT**

"A DOLT gets the VOLTS."

- ❑ The frustrated teacher said he had a class full of DOLTS.

- ❑ Only a DOLT would put his shoes on backward.

- ❑ Jonathan felt DOLTISH because he was the only student to fail gym class.

CLONE

(klohn) *n.*
an exact duplicate
Link: CONE

"CLONE CONES."

- ❏ The scientist CLONED a lab rat.
- ❏ Identical twins may be called CLONES.
- ❏ McDonalds restaurants are CLONES of each other.

CARNIVORE

(KAR ni vour) *n.*
a flesh-eating animal
Link: **DINOSAUR**

"CARNIVORE DINOSAURS."

- ❑ The most famous of the **CARNIVOROUS** dinosaurs was the Tyrannosaurus Rex.

- ❑ Jan jokingly calls her brother a **CARNIVORE** because all he wants for dinner is meat.

- ❑ Alligators and crocodiles are **CARNIVORES**.

DESPOT

(DES puht) *n.*

an absolute ruler

Link: **THIS POT**

"THIS POT is the DESPOT."

- ❑ The DESPOT declared his birthday a national holiday.

- ❑ My big brother thinks he is the DESPOT of the family; he is always bossing everyone around.

- ❑ Fidel Castro is the DESPOTIC ruler of Cuba.

COURIER

(KUUR ee ur) *n.*

a messenger

Link: **CARRY HER**

"The CARRY HER COURIER Service."

- ❑ The COURIER delivered an important letter from the general.

- ❑ Frederick works as a COURIER for United Parcel Service.

- ❑ The spy acted as a COURIER, carrying secret information between the United States and Europe.

SPECTER
(SPEK ter) *n.*
a ghost or phantom
Link: **SPECTACLES**

"A SPECTER with SPECTACLES."

- ❏ After the kids yelled "trick or treat," a SPECTER appeared in the door causing them to run away without any candy.

- ❏ As the lights came up on stage, a SPECTER seemed to materialize from no where.

- ❏ The SPECTER of Christmas Past is the most terrifying to Ebenezer Scrooge in Dickens' <u>A Christmas Carole</u>.

MOGUL
(MOH guhl) *n.*
a very rich or powerful person; a magnate
Link: **SEA GULL**

"A SEA GULL MOGUL."

- ❏ Howard Hughes was a famous MOGUL who was rarely seen in public.

- ❏ Leslie's dream is to marry a MOGUL, have ten kids, and live in luxury.

- ❏ After forming Microsoft, Bill Gates became the most recognized computer MOGUL.

REVIEW #15: Match the word with its definition.

1. iconoclast – (kind to the past)
2. sage – (page)
3. nemesis – (my sis)
4. dolt – (volt)
5. clone – (cone)
6. carnivore – (dinosaur)
7. despot – (pot)
8. courier – (carry her)
9. specter – (spectacles)
10. mogul – (sea gull)

a. a stupid person
b. a meat eater
c. a rich or powerful person
d. one who attacks tradition
e. an exact duplicate
f. a ghost or phantom
g. an unbeatable opponent
h. an absolute ruler
i. a messenger
j. a person of wisdom

Fill in the blanks with the appropriate word. The word form may need changing.

1. The _____ declared his birthday a national holiday.
2. Native America tribes regarded their medicine man as a _____ with special healing powers.
3. After forming Microsoft, Bill Gates became the most recognized computer _____.
4. Young voters were attracted to the candidate's _____ platform.
5. Lex Luther considers Superman his _____.
6. Alligators and crocodiles are _____.
7. The frustrated teacher said he had a class full of _____.
8. The _____ delivered an important letter from the general.
9. Brad felt the cold chill of a _____ after entering the haunted house.
10. The scientist _____ a lab rat.

179

BOVINE

(BOH vyne) *adj.*

of, relating to, or resembling an animal such
as an ox, cow or buffalo; solid; dull

Link: **VINE**

"A BOVINE on a VINE."

❑ The BOVINE features of the man scared the
children.

❑ Sue came to the party and sat in the corner
reading a book as she BOVINELY ignored all the
guests.

❑ The BOVINITY of Michael's personality changed
to that of zestful enthusiasm only when the
subject of beetles and cockroaches came up.

SUPINE

(soo PYNE) *adj.*
lying on the back with the face
turned upward; inclined

Link: **SPINE**

"Lying SUPINE on the SPINE."

❏ When the investigators arrived, the body was still SUPINE in the middle of the living room floor.

❏ The chiropractor had Jill lie in a SUPINE position so he could adjust her neck.

❏ The referee stopped the fight when the boxer lay on the mat in a SUPINE position and could not get up.

ASININE
(AS ih nine) *adj.*

silly; stupid

Link: ASS OF MINE

"This ASS OF MINE is ASININE."

❑ My sister gave up working in a mental hospital because she could no longer deal with ASININE behavior.

❑ Adam is usually a nice guy, but sometimes he is so ASININE no one can stand him.

❑ The phone solicitor asked so many ASININE questions that I finally hung up.

MARITIME

(mar ih TYME) *adj.*
near the sea; concerning with
shipping or navigation

Link: **MERRY TIME**

*"MARITIME sailors having a
MERRY TIME."*

- ❏ While in our nation's capitol, we visited the MARITIME War Museum.

- ❏ Rick's desire is to become a MARITIME lawyer.

- ❏ Jacksonville is a MARITIME city in Florida.

SUBLIME

(suh BLYME) *adj.*

impressive; inspiring awe; majestic

Link: SUB LIME

*"The Navy's new SUB LIME
was SUBLIME."*

- ❏ The lecturer had something to offer each of his listeners; he was a master of moving his speech from the ridiculous to the SUBLIME.

- ❏ The SUBLIME melody worked itself throughout the entire musical.

- ❏ The priest's SUBLIME voice made him the object of admiration in his parish.

SERENE
(se REEN) *adj.*
clear; calm; tranquil
Link: **SCENE**

*"Teachers often daydream
of a SERENE SCENE."*

- ❑ The <u>Mona Lisa</u> has a SERENE smile.

- ❑ Game day dawned with a SERENE sky.

- ❑ The family goes to the beach whenever they need SERENITY.

FOREBODE
(for BODE) *v.*
to predict or foretell
Link: FOUR BONES

*"The gypsy FOREBODED FOUR BONES
in Rex's future."*

- ❏ In ancient Greece it was believed that a sage could FOREBODE the future.

- ❏ A FOREBODING rain began working its way toward us. (A FOREBODING is the feeling that something is about to happen.)

- ❏ The policeman's purple face and clenched fists FOREBODE his anger.

BOMBASTIC

(bom BAS tik) *adj.*
high sounding; use of language
without much real meaning

Link: **BOMBS IN A BASKET**

"The President's speech was so BOMBASTIC, he was spitting BOMBS IN A BASKET."

❏ Politicians are often times full of BOMBAST and bluster.

❏ Take the BOMBAST away from the lawyer's court arguments, and you would have little but outright lies.

❏ Some people debate by shouting down their opponents with BOMBASTIC language.

WINNOW
(WIN oh) *v.*
to rid of undesirable parts
Link: **MINNOW**

"WINNOWING MINNOWS."

❑ The military attempts to WINNOW out those who are not officer material.

❑ When the children were allowed to choose their own groups, a natural WINNOWING occurred.

❑ The wild dogs WINNOWED the offal trying to get some nutrition.

SPAWN
(spahn) *v.*
to give rise to; to produce
in large numbers
Link: **YAWN**

"A SPAWNED YAWN."

- ❑ Salmon always return to their native streams at SPAWNING time.

- ❑ Joe's negative outlook SPAWNED hard feelings in his teammates.

- ❑ The flu outbreak SPAWNED major attendance problems at the school.

REVIEW #16: Match the word with its definition.

1. bovine – (vine)
2. supine – (spine)
3. asinine – (ass of mine)
4. maritime – (merry time)
5. sublime – (sub lime)
6. serene – (scene)
7. forebode – (four bones)
8. bombastic – (bombs in a basket)
9. winnow – (minnow)
10. spawn – (yawn)

a. inspiring awe
b. resembling a cow
c. to predict or foretell
d. pompous speech or writing
e. calm; tranquil
f. to rid of undesirable parts
g. silly, stupid
h. lying on the back
i. to give rise to
j. concerning with shipping

**Fill in the blanks with the appropriate word. The word
form may need changing.**

1. When the investigators arrived, the body was still _____ in the middle of the living room floor.

2. Game day dawned with a _____ sky.

3. While in our nation's capitol, we visited the _____ War Museum.

4. The _____ features of the man scared the children.

5. Some people debate by shouting down their opponents with _____ language.

6. The drama class's performance of "Grease" was _____.

7. The flu outbreak _____ major attendance problems at the school.

8. The phone solicitor asked so many _____ questions that I finally hung up.

9. The military attempts to _____ out those who are not officer material.

10. In ancient Greece it was believed that a sage could _____ the future.

190

PRODIGIOUS
(pra dij us) *adj.*
enormous in size, quantity, degree;
marvelous, amazing
Link: **DISH**

"A PRODIGIOUS DISH."

- ❑ The construction of the Panama Canal was a PRODIGIOUS undertaking.

- ❑ The trainer managed to escape a ferociously PRODIGIOUS lion by climbing a tree.

- ❑ The PRODIGIOUSNESS of marathon runners who run twenty-six miles in a few hours is truly extraordinary.

BOOR

(buur) *n.*
a rude person; someone that is
unrefined

Link: **BOAR**

"Dan was a real BOOR at parties."

- ❏ His BOORISH manners at prom made everyone uncomfortable.

- ❏ She BOORISHLY asked for a take home bag at the wedding reception.

- ❏ Jake's BOORISHNESS was apparent as soon as he started slurping soup and eating salad with his fingers.

PANACHE
(pa NASH) *n.*
dashing elegance of manner or style
Link: MUSTACHE

*"Sir Charles' MUSTACHE is a
symbol of his PANACHE."*

- ❑ Eric entered the room with PANACHE, wearing his new tux, Rolex watch, and $500 shoes.

- ❑ It was evident by the woman's PANACHE that she was a member of the royal family.

- ❑ Mom was impressed with my PANACHE after I returned home from finishing school.

FORBEARANCE

(for BAYR ans) *adj.*

patience

Link: **FOUR PARENTS**

"FOUR PARENTS exhibiting FORBEARANCE."

☐ Teachers must FORBEAR when they deal with unruly students.

☐ The hunter showed great FORBEARANCE by sitting in the tree stand all day long.

☐ Social workers must possess FORBEARANCE to deal with their difficult clients.

AGOG

(ah gog) *adj.*
highly excited by eagerness
Link: EGGNOG

"Our dog is AGOG for EGGNOG."

- ❑ Michelle was AGOG when her mom said she could spend the night at her friend's house.

- ❑ Betty and Laura are always AGOG on Christmas morning.

- ❑ Jim sat AGOG when his name was announced as the winner of the Pulitzer Prize.

FORTHRIGHT
(FOWRTH ryt) *adj.*
frank; going straight to the point
Link: **FOURTH FROM THE RIGHT**

*"The soldier FOURTH FROM THE RIGHT
was FORTHRIGHT."*

❑ Whenever I want a FORTHRIGHT opinion, I always ask my two year old son.

❑ The boss asked everyone to be FORTHRIGHT at the company meeting.

❑ When Kathy asked Mark if her dress made her look fat, she wasn't expecting his answer to be so FORTHRIGHT.

PROFOUND

(pro FOWND) *adj.*

intellectually deep or penetrating; reaching to, rising from, or effecting the depth's of one's nature

Link: **TOES FOUND**

"The TOES of King Two TOES Kahmin was a PROFOUND discovery."

❑ Many psychologists believe violence on television and in film has a PROFOUND effect on our behavior toward others.

❑ Advertising has a PROFOUND effect on the failure or success of many products.

❑ Although they at first seem simple, Emily Dickinson's poems are PROFOUND in their philosophy.

FIASCO
(fee AS koh) *n.*
a complete or humiliating failure
Link: **TABASCO**

"A TABASCO FIASCO."

- ❑ The children's plan to release all the animals at the Humane Society was an utter FIASCO.

- ❑ Our government has been involved in numerous FIASCOES which will go down in history.

- ❑ Teresa ordered $300 worth of Girl Scout cookies and her parents had to pay for the FIASCO.

DOLEFUL
(DOHL ful) *adj.*
sorrowful; melancholy
Link: **BOWL FULL**

"Billy was DOLEFUL because he had to eat a BOWL FULL of split pea soup."

❑ The DOLEFUL expression on the dog's face suggested he thought he had been deserted by his owner.

❑ A DOLEFUL procession of mourners followed the hearse to the cemetery.

❑ When the doctor arrived to see her ailing husband, Jim's wife DOLEFULLY opened the door to let him in.

OPAQUE
(oh PAYK) *adj.*
having no luster; dull; hard to understand
Link: **FAKE**

"This "diamond" is OPAQUE; it's a FAKE."

- ❏ Jean put an OPAQUE blue glaze on her ceramic teapot.

- ❏ The photographer's use of OPAQUE lighting enhanced the family portrait.

- ❏ The ballerina's tights were an OPAQUE pink, revealing none of her skin.

REVIEW #17: Match the word with its definition.

1. prodigious – (dish)
2. boor – (boar)
3. panache – (mustache)
4. forbearance – (four parents)
5. agog – (eggnog)
6. forthright – (4th from the right)
7. profound – (toes found)
8. fiasco – (tabasco)
9. doleful – (bowl full)
10. opaque – (fake)

a. straight to the point
b. intellectually deep
c. a rude person
d. dashing elegance of manner or style
e. enormous; amazing
f. sorrowful; melancholy
g. patience
h. having no luster; dull
i. a complete failure
j. eager; highly excited

Fill in the blanks with the appropriate word. The word form may need changing.

1. A _____ procession of mourners followed the hearse to the cemetery.

2. Eric entered the room with _____, wearing his new tux, Rolex watch, and $500 shoe.

3. His _____ manners at the prom made everyone uncomfortable.

4. The children's plan to release all the animals at the Humane Society was an utter _____.

5. The construction of the Panama Canal was a _____ undertaking.

6. Advertising has a _____ effect on the failure or success of many products.

7. The boss asked everyone to be _____ at the company meeting.

8. Elizabeth and Laura are always _____ on Christmas morning.

9. The photographer's use of _____ lighting enhanced the family portrait.

10. The hunter showed great _____ by sitting in the tree stand all day long.

ANNALS
(an ulz) *n.*
descriptive record; history
Link: HANDLES

"Putting HANDLES on the sculptured ANNALS."

- ❑ The championship team of 1963 has gone down in the school's ANNALS as the best team of the century.

- ❑ Books having to do with the history of something are often referred to as ANNALS.

- ❑ The ANNALS of history should teach us how to avoid war.

TOME

(tohm) *n.*
a large book
Link: HOME

"A bookworm's HOME is a TOME."

- The witch pulled a TOME from the shelf and began looking for a spell.

- Thank goodness encyclopedias are now on CD-rom so we don't have to find room for all those TOMES in our house.

- The professor carried the Shakespearean TOME as if it were a Bible.

CATARACT

(KAT ah rakt) *n.*
a large waterfall; a deluge;
an eye abnormality

Link: **CADILLAC**

*"John preferred going over the CATARACT
in his CADILLAC ."*

- ☐ Niagara Falls is probably the most well-known CATARACT in North America.

- ☐ The storm flooded the town with a CATARACT of rain.

- ☐ The old dog developed cloudy CATARACTS on both his eyes.

BOOTY

(BOO tee) *n.*
loot; the spoils of war; goods or property
seized by force; a valuable prize
Link: **BOOTS**

"Tex keeps his BOOTY in his BOOTS."

- ❑ Some servicemen during World War II felt they were entitled to all the BOOTY they could capture.

- ❑ Pirates kept their BOOTY in chests which they sometimes buried.

- ❑ The burglars were apprehended before they could make off with the BOOTY.

ANIMATED

(an eh MATE ed) *adj.*
having life; alive; filled with
activity, vigor, or spirit

Link: **ANNA MADE IT**

"ANNA became ANIMATED when she finally MADE IT."

- ☐ Bill was an ANIMATED speaker on any subject that interested him.

- ☐ Liz played the violin with intense ANIMATION.

- ☐ Tina became highly ANIMATED when she heard she was voted the "most likely to succeed."

JETSAM
(JET sem) *n.*
cargo or equipment thrown overboard to lighten
an imperiled vessel; discarded odds and ends
Link: **JETS**

"The JETS became JETSAM."

❏ Because we were overloaded, we had to dump
some of our JETSAM in order not to sink.

❏ Jessica found a piece of blue glass on the water's
edge, but her father explained it was merely
JETSAM.

❏ After a storm, JETSAM is often discovered on the
beach.

PORTAL
(POR tul) *n.*
an entrance, door or gate
Link: **PORTHOLE**

"A PORTHOLE PORTAL."

❏ As we stepped through the PORTAL of the Sistine Chapel, everyone was awestruck.

❏ Dante writes about the PORTALS of death in his The Divine Comedy.

❏ The space travelers stepped through the PORTAL into another dimension.

THRONG

(throng) *n.*
a large group of people gathered
closely together
Link: **SONG**

"The THRONG broke into SONG."

- ❏ When the Pope visited the United States, an admiring THRONG gathered at every major city.

- ❏ THRONGS of revelers gather at Times Square in New York City on New Year's Eve.

- ❏ The assassins THRONGED around Caesar before they murdered him.

BARRAGE

(bah RAHZH) *n.*

a curtain of artillery fire; any overwhelming
attack, as of words or blows

Link: **GARAGE**

*"Our GARAGE was BARRAGED with
eggs on Halloween."*

- ❑ When Maria walked in the sorority house after
  her date, she was BARRAGED with questions.

- ❑ The attempt to attack was met by a BARRAGE of
  gunfire.

- ❑ The boxer backed his opponent into the corner
  and BARRAGED him with punches.

ELITE

(i LEET) *n.*
the best or most skilled
members of a group
Link: FEET

"The ELITE wine makers have big FEET."

❑ Members of the school's academic teams are among the educational ELITE.

❑ The city was defended by an ELITE corps of soldiers.

❑ An ELITIST is a snob; to be ELITIST is to be snobby.

REVIEW #18: **Match the word with its definition.**

1. annals – (handles)
2. tome – (home)
3. cataract – (Cadillac)
4. booty – (boots)
5. animated – (Anna made it)
6. jetsam – (jets)
7. portal – (port hole)
8. throng – (song)
9. barrage – (garage)
10. elite – (feet)

a. an entrance, door or gate
b. having life, vigor
c. a large book
d. a curtain of artillery fire
e. a large waterfall
f. objects thrown overboard
g. history
h. the best of a group
i. loot; property seized
j. a large group

Fill in the blanks with the appropriate word. The word form may need changing.

1. When the Pope visited the United States, an admiring _____ gathered at every major city.

2. Bill was an _____ speaker on any subject that interested him.

3. Niagara Falls is probably the most well-known _____ in North America.

4. The championship team of 1963 has gone down in the school's _____ as the best team of the century.

5. The city was defended by an _____ corps of soldiers.

6. Pirates kept their _____ in chests which they sometimes buried.

7. The army's attempt to attack was met by a _____ of gunfire.

8. After a storm, _____ is often discovered on the beach.

9. The witch pulled a _____ from the shelf and began looking for a spell.

10. The space travelers stepped through the _____ into another dimension.

FETTER

(FET ur) *v.*
to restrain; to hamper
Link: **FEATHER**

"A FETTERED FEATHER."

❑ The prisoners were FETTERED by shackles around their ankles.

❑ The cowboy FETTERED his horse so it would be there when he wanted to go home.

❑ Since Joe's parents were out of town, he invited his friends over for some UNFETTERED fun.

TORPID

(TOR pid) *adj.*

dormant; inactive; lethargic

Link: **TORPEDO**

"TORPID TORPEDOES."

❑ The teacher could not understand the boy's TORPID reactions until she learned that he could not understand English.

❑ During winter, bears sleep TORPIDLY in caves.

❑ Volcanoes may be TORPID for centuries and one day suddenly erupt.

TORRID
(TOR id) *adj.*
intensely hot; burning;
passionate; rapid
Link: **POOR ED**

"POOR ED never survived the TORRID desert."

❑ The TORRID heat and wind are what led to the Dust Bowl of the 1930's.

❑ Many romance novels contain TORRID love affairs.

❑ The salesman TORRIDLY spoke to the group hoping to sell them a time share in paradise.

PINGUID

(pen gwed) *adj.*

fat

Link: PENGUIN

"A PINGUID PENGUIN."

- ❑ The PINGUID egg roll left a greasy stain on the paper plate.

- ❑ The PINGUID roast splattered all over the oven.

- ❑ The PINGUIDITY of British food tends to put me off.

DISHEVEL
(di SHEV ul) *v.*
to make untidy; to disarrange
the hair or clothing of
Link: SHOVEL

*"Tommy DISHEVELED his aunt
with his SHOVEL."*

❑ Andrea's hair became DISHEVELED in the strong
breeze.

❑ After the hurricane, our yard was DISHEVELED
with broken branches and debris.

❑ From the looks of Bryan's DISHEVELED desk,
one would think he is a disorganized person.

NETTLE

(NET l) *v.*

to irritate; vex

Link: SETTLE

"Mosquitoes NETTLE when they SETTLE."

- ❑ My little brother always seems to NETTLE me.

- ❑ Hip Hop music NETTLES my parents.

- ❑ The noise NETTLED its way from the room next door.

MOTTLE
(MOT el) *v.*
to mark with spots or blotches of
different shades or colors
Link: **BOTTLE**

*"The rare MOTTLED mouse caught
in a BOTTLE."*

❑ The Dalmatian's MOTTLED fur is its salient trait.

❑ After years of sunbathing, Jean's skin became MOTTLED.

❑ The soldier's MOTTLED uniform was designed for camouflage.

PRATTLE

(PRAT l) *v.*

to babble; to talk meaninglessly

Link: RATTLE

AND MY DEAR, I TOLD OSCAR IF HE'S COMING LATE FOR DINNER HE COULD EAT COLD FROGS FOR ALL I CARED. A POOR HOUSE SNAKE WORKS HER RATTLES TO THE BONES AND HER HUSBAND DOESN'T APPRECIATE HER. WHY A MAN WHO DOES THAT IS NO BETTER THAN A SNAKE IN THE GRASS.

"PRATTLING RATTLEsnakes."

❑ Mary and Leslie PRATTLE on about everyone in the neighborhood.

❑ The three year old PRATTLED for hours although no one understood what she was saying.

❑ My mother PRATTLES so endlessly I barely can understand what she is talking about.

BALK
(bawk) *v.*
to stop short and refuse to proceed
Link: **WALK**

"The pirate BALKED at WALKING the plank."

❑ Marcie was injured when her horse BALKED at the last jump in the steeplechase.

❑ The judge BALKED the hearing until order was restored in his court.

❑ The warden took efforts to BALK the escape attempt of the prisoners.

CURB

(kurb) *v.*

to control or check

Link: **HERB**

"HERB could not CURB his love of flying."

❑ Weight Watchers' mission is to help corpulent people CURB their appetites.

❑ She wore a patch to try to CURB her addiction to nicotine.

❑ By making them raise their hands, the new teacher CURBED her students' tendency to shout out the answers.

REVIEW #19: **Match the word with its definition.**

1. fetter – (feather)   a. fat
2. torpid – (torpedo)   b. to irritate; vex
3. torrid – (poor Ed)   c. to restrain; hamper
4. pinguid – (penguin)   d. to control or check
5. dishevel – (shovel)   e. to talk meaninglessly
6. nettle – (settle)   f. intensely hot
7. mottle – (bottle)   g. to make untidy
8. prattle – (rattle)   h. dormant; lethargic
9. balk – (walk)   i. to stop short
10. curb – (Herb)   j. to mark with spots

**Fill in the blanks with the appropriate word. The word
form may need changing.**

1. Volcanoes may be _____ for centuries and one day
   suddenly erupt.

2. Weight Watcher's mission is to help corpulent people
   _____ their appetites.

3. Marcie was injured when her horse _____ at the last
   jump in the steeplechase.

4. The _____ heat and wind are what led to the Dust Bowl
   of the 1930's.

5. The prisoners were _____ by shackles around their
   ankles.

6. The soldier's _____ uniform was designed for
   camouflage.

7. Andrea's hair became _____ in the strong breeze.

8. My little brother always seems to _____ me.

9. The _____ roast was to big to fit in the oven.

10. The three year old _____ for hours although no one
    understood what she was saying.

223

ASSAIL
(ah SAIL) *v.*
to attack violently
Link: **SAIL**

"A ship's SAIL being ASSAILED."

- ❑ The debaters ASSAILED each other with facts, each hoping to persuade the judges to see things his way.

- ❑ While the defendant claims he did not ASSAIL the claimant, he did have bruises to prove otherwise.

- ❑ Music ASSAILED our ears as we walked into the concert hall.

QUAIL

(kwayl) *v.*
to shrink with fear; to cower;
to lose heart and courage

Link: **QUAIL (bird)**

"A QUAILING QUAIL."

- ❑ The quarterback did not QUAIL as the defensive line ran to crush him.

- ❑ A leader is one who does not QUAIL in the face of adversity.

- ❑ The previously beaten dog QUAILED each time his new owner raised his hand.

DWELL

(dwel) *v.*

to make one's home; reside; to focus attention on; to speak or write about at length

Link: **HILL**

"Ants DWELL in a HILL."

❑ Bruce is a contractor of apartment DWELLINGS.

❑ That book DWELLS on the need for better schools.

❑ Don't DWELL on the negative, think of the positive.

QUELL

(kwel) *v.*
to extinguish; to put down
or suppress by force

Link: QUILT

"Grandma QUELLED the fire with a QUILT."

❑ The mother attempted to QUELL the infant's cries by singing a lullaby.

❑ The National Guard was sent in to try to QUELL the rioting crowd.

❑ A mob stabbed Caesar in an attempt to QUELL his power.

QUAFF
(kwaf) *v.*
to drink heartily
Link: GIRAFFE

"A QUAFFING GIRAFFE."

- ❏ I offered her a sip, but she QUAFFED the entire soda.

- ❏ Fraternity parties often involve the QUAFFING of large quantities of beverages.

- ❏ Many of the senior citizens were guilty of QUAFFING far too much food and drink at the early bird special.

ESTRANGE
(eh STRANJ) *v.*
to alienate; to treat as a stranger; to turn an
affectionate attitude into an indifferent or
unfriendly one
Link: **STRANGE**

*"Nancy became ESTRANGED from her husband
because he was so STRANGE."*

❏ Lawrence feared his candid views of the company
would ESTRANGE him from his coworkers.

❏ Hardly recognizing anyone, Ed felt ESTRANGED
from his old high school classmates during his
25th reunion.

❏ The governor stated that capital punishment does
not deter crime, and in so doing ESTRANGED
himself from many of his erstwhile supporters.

DISCONCERT

(dis cun SURT) *v.*

to disturb the composure of; upset; to frustrate
(as a plan) by throwing into disorder

Link: **THIS CONCERT**

*"THIS CONCERT is DISCONCERTING
to my father."*

❑ Some students find it very DISCONCERTING to
listen to music while studying.

❑ A baby may be unaffected by loud noises while
the simplest sound may be DISCONCERTING.

❑ I don't mean to DISCONCERT your plans, but I
can't attend your party on Saturday.

ANNEX
(an NEKS) *v.*
to add or attach
Link: **NECKS**

"An ANNEXED NECK."

- ❑ The wedding reception was held in the ANNEX of the church.

- ❑ Because the school was growing so quickly, a portable room was used as an ANNEX.

- ❑ The ANNEXATION being built adjacent to the hospital is nearly complete.

ESPOUSE
(eh SPOWZ) *v.*
to adopt; to support
Link: **SPOUSE**

"Harold's SPOUSE ESPOUSED a large family

- ❑ I ESPOUSE the idea that we eat dessert before dinner.

- ❑ The candidate for governor ESPOUSED a one cent sales tax to build a new stadium.

- ❑ Because Barbara was always ready to ESPOUSE students' privileges, she was elected senior class president.

REPROACH
(ri PROHCH) *v.*
to express disapproval of
Link: COACH

"The COACH REPROACHED his team."

❑ Jessica's teacher wrote a recommendation for her because her work had always been above REPROACH.

❑ While on trial the criminal REPROACHINGLY named others so he would not have to take the punishment alone.

❑ Although he realized his behavior was not beyond REPROACH, he didn't think it was bad enough for him to be suspended from school.

233

REVIEW #20: Match the word with its definition.

1. assail – (sail)
2. quail – (quail)
3. dwell – (hill)
4. quell – (quilt)
5. quaff – (giraffe)
6. estrange – (strange)
7. disconcert – (this concert)
8. annex – (add necks)
9. espouse – (spouse)
10. reproach – (coach)

a. to shrink in fear
b. to drink heartily
c. to add or attach
d. to make one's home
e. to express disapproval of
f. to adopt or support
g. to attack violently
h. to upset or frustrate
i. to suppress or put down
j. to alienate

Fill in the blanks with the appropriate word. The word form may need changing.

1. The National Guard was sent in to try to _____ the rioting crowd.

2. Jessica's teacher wrote a recommendation for her because her work had always been above _____.

3. While the defendant claims he did not _____ the claimant, he did have bruises to prove otherwise.

4. The candidate for governor _____ a one cent sales tax to build a new stadium.

5. Bats _____ in caves.

6. I offered her a sip, but she _____ the entire soda.

7. Lawrence feared his candid views of the company would _____ him from his coworkers.

8. A leader is one who does not _____ in the face of adversity.

9. Because the school was growing so quickly, a portable room was used as an _____.

10. I don't mean to _____ your plans, but I can't attend your party on Saturday.

PACIFIST
(PAS ih fist) *n.*
one who is in opposition
of war or violence
Link: **FIST**

"A PACIFIST never uses his FIST."

❏ Julie is such a PACIFIST; she doesn't even like violent movies.

❏ The PACIFISTS protested the boxing match by lying on the mat and refusing to move.

❏ Because of Brad's PACIFISTIC personality, he refused to get into a fight.

BEQUEST

(bi KWEST) *n.*

something left to someone in a will

Link: GO WEST

"Joe's last BEQUEST was to GO WEST."

❑ If your parents leave you their house, the house is a BEQUEST from them to you.

❑ Hortensia's jewelry was a BEQUEST from her mother.

❑ (BEQUEATH is a verb meaning the act of leaving something in a will.) Tim's father BEQUEATHED his ring to his son who was pleased with the BEQUEST.

MANIFEST
(MAN ih fest) *adj.*
clearly apparent to the sight
or understanding; obvious
Link: **MAN IN VEST**

*"It is MANIFEST that the MAN IN
the VEST is the butler.*

❑ Rebecca's flu symptoms were MANIFEST, yet the doctor could do nothing.

❑ There is MANIFEST danger of lighting a match near a gas pump.

❑ Ryan was MANIFESTED with a sense of urgency when he discovered he was already 30 minutes late for his appointment.

ROTE
(roht) *n.*
a memorizing process using routine or
repetition, often without comprehension
Link: **ROPE**

"ROTE ROPING."

❑ Foreign languages are no longer taught by ROTE.

❑ Although Allison had not been in a church for years, by ROTE she knew how to do everything correctly.

❑ The teacher taught as if by ROTE; a computer would have had more personality.

MORASS

(meh RAS) *n.*
anything that hinders, traps or overwhelms;
low-lying, soggy ground

Link: MOLASSES

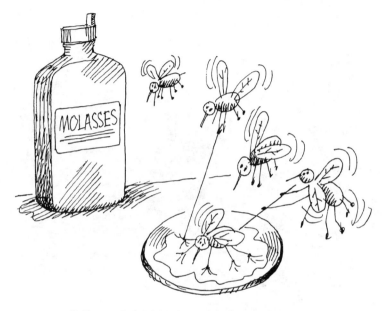

"The MOLASSES created a MORASS."

- ❑ The MORASS surrounding the castle was ineffective during the dry season.

- ❑ The jeep sank deep into the MORASS and could go no further.

- ❑ The MORASS was too wet for gardening so we brought in some fill dirt.

REIGN

(rayn) *n.*
the exercise or possession of
supreme power

Link: RAIN

"Frogs REIGN in the RAIN."

- ❑ Queen Elizabeth has REIGNED over England since the 1950's.

- ❑ Many believe the king's REIGN was strikingly enlightened.

- ❑ The new winner of the Miss America pageant began her REIGN by taking the crown of last year's winner.

BROUHAHA

(BROO hah hah) *n.*
an uproar; hubbub

Link: **BREW HA HA**

"The witches created a real BROUHAHA while stirring their BREW."

❑ What began as a quiet party, suddenly turned into a BROUHAHA.

❑ A BROUHAHA started in the government offices when a threatening e-mail was received.

❑ My mother warned me that if the sleep-over turned into a BROUHAHA, she would send all my friends home.

WRATH

(rath) *n.*

extreme or violent rage

Link: **RATS**

"Monica revealing her WRATH for RATS."

- ❑ The Puritans feared the WRATH of God above all else.

- ❑ After she had been caught cheating, Judi awaited the WRATH of the assistant principal.

- ❑ Her eyes were full of WRATH as she glared at his new girlfriend.

ZENITH
(ZEE nith) *n.*
the peak; the highest point
Link: **BENEATH IT**

"When the Sun is at its ZENITH, you are directly BENEATH IT."

❑ The sun reached its ZENITH at about noon.

❑ Nick Faldo claimed that winning The Masters Tournament was the ZENITH of his golfing career.

❑ After the whale broke the water, he reached his ZENITH before he started his descent.

SLAKE
(slayk) *v.*
to quench; to satisfy a craving
Link: **LAKE**

"Larry SLAKED his thirst in the LAKE."

- During halftime, the quarterback tried to SLAKE his thirst by drinking Gatorade.

- Ben read everything he could in an attempt to SLAKE his desire for knowledge.

- Jeannie SLAKED her nicotine craving by going outdoors to have a cigarette.

REVIEW #21: Match the word with its definition.

1. pacifist – (fist)
2. bequest – (go west)
3. manifest – (man in vest)
4. rote – (rope)
5. morass – (molasses)
6. reign – (rain)
7. brouhaha – (brew ha ha)
8. wrath – (rats)
9. zenith – (beneath it)
10. slake – (lake)

a. an uproar
b. the exercise of supreme power
c. one who opposes violence
d. extreme or violent rage
e. to quench
f. soggy ground
g. clearly apparent
h. something left in a will
i. a memorizing process
j. the peak or highest point

Fill in the blanks with the appropriate word. The word form may need changing.

1. Queen Elizabeth has _____ over England since the 1950's.

2. Foreign languages are no longer taught by _____.

3. The jeep sank deep into the _____ and could go no further.

4. Rebecca's flu symptoms were _____, yet the doctor could do nothing.

5. Julie is such a _____; she doesn't even like violent movies.

6. The sun reached its _____ at about noon.

7. Her eyes were full of _____ as she glared at his new girlfriend.

8. Hortensia's jewelry was a _____ from her mother.

9. During halftime, the quarterback tried to _____ his thirst by drinking Gatorade.

10. What began as a quiet party, suddenly turned into a _____.

245

BEDLAM

(BED lum) *n.*

a place or scene of noisy uproar
and confusion

Link: **BED LAMB**

"BEDLAM in the LAMB'S BED."

❑ Before the new teacher took over, there was total BEDLAM in the classroom.

❑ It was BEDLAM behind stage until the curtain went up and the play began.

❑ Following the championship soccer match, the stadium was in a state of BEDLAM.

PREHENSILE
(pri HEN sil) *adj.*
adapted for grasping or holding
Link: **UTENSIL**

*"The monkey's PREHENSILE tail
held the UTENSIL."*

❏ The elephant uses its trunk in a PREHENSILE manner.

❏ Because of our thumbs, humans are much better at PREHENSILE movements than are most other mammals.

❏ The PREHENSIBILITY of that eagle is amazing; who would have ever thought it could carry such a large fish.

DOUR

(dowr) *adj.*

severe; gloomy; stern

Link: **FLOWER**

"A DOUR FLOWER."

- ❑ The garbage collector was a DOUR older man who never had a kind word for anyone.

- ❑ When the Legionnaire begged the Arab for water, the Arab DOURLY replied he barely had enough for his camel.

- ❑ The barren DOURNESS of the infertile land on their farm made it almost impossible for Tim's family to make a living as farmers.

TAUT

(tawt) *adj.*
stretched tight; tidy
Link: CAUGHT

*"Eric CAUGHT a lot of fish because
his line was TAUT."*

- ❏ The sailor pulled the lines TAUT, so he could sail against the wind.

- ❏ As he stared down the snout of the bull, the toreador's muscles became as TAUT as piano wire.

- ❏ The commander was proud that he ran such a TAUT ship.

RIFE

(ryfe) *adj.*

abundant; great in number or amount

Link: **LIFE**

"The ocean is RIFE with LIFE."

- ❏ The new, tough administrator was sent to take over the hospital which was RIFE with problems.

- ❏ When I got my paper back, it was covered with red ink; the teacher said it was RIFE with errors.

- ❏ Disease is RIFE throughout sections of India.

INDOLENCE
(IN doh lents) *adj.*
lazy
Link: **ON THE FENCE**

"The INDOLENT crows sat ON THE FENCE."

❑ Christopher may get by in high school, but college professors will never put up with such INDOLENCE.

❑ The Puritans had no use for INDOLENCE as is clear in their Work Ethic.

❑ Because his parents are such hard workers, Kevin's INDOLENCE in school came as a shock to them.

INCONTROVERTIBLE

(in kon trah VUR tih bul) adj.
not able to be "turned against" or
disputed; certain; indisputable

Link: **CONVERTIBLE**

*"It's INCONTROVERTIBLE that beauty queens ride
in CONVERTIBLES ."*

❑ The suspect's fingerprints on the window were
considered INCONTROVERTIBLE evidence of
his participation in the robbery.

❑ Christina INCONTROVERTIBILITY believes in
herself.

❑ It is INCONTROVERTIBLE that two plus two
equals four.

BENIGHTED

(be NI tid) *adj.*
being in a state of intellectual darkness;
ignorant; unenlightened

Link: **KNIGHT**

"A BENIGHTED KNIGHT."

❑ Many BENIGHTED people became enlightened during the Renaissance.

❑ Cameron had never read a book but was so BENIGHTED that he did not realize he would never be accepted into Harvard.

❑ He BENIGHTEDLY asked the professor how much she would take to give him an A in her class.

253

REQUISITE
(REK wu zit) *adj.*
requirement
Link: **WRECK SIT**

"It's not REQUISITE to SIT on the WRECK until the police arrive."

❏ On the first day of class the teacher explained that doing our homework is not only important, it is REQUISITE.

❏ Successfully completing Latin I is REQUISITE to taking Latin II.

❏ One REQUISITE for admission to college is high SAT scores.

SHUNT

(shunt) *v.*
to move or turn aside; to evade
by putting aside or ignoring
Link: **RUNT**

"A SHUNTED RUNT."

- ❏ The crash was caused by failure of the trainman to SHUNT the train onto the proper rails.

- ❏ Nick was so upset by Tom's previous behavior that he SHUNTED him when Tom tried to shake his hand.

- ❏ The running back dashed down the field SHUNTING right and left to avoid the tacklers.

REVIEW #22: Match the word with its definition.

1. bedlam – (bed lamb)
2. prehensile – (utensil)
3. dour – (flower)
4. taut – (caught)
5. rife – (life)
6. indolence – (on the fence)
7. incontrovertible – (convertible)
8. benighted – (knight)
9. requisite – (wreck sit)
10. shunt – (runt)

a. lazy
b. stretched tight; tidy
c. indisputable; certain
d. severe; gloomy; stern
e. to evade by putting aside
f. abundant
g. adapted for grasping or holding
h. a place of noisy uproar
i. requirement
j. ignorant

Fill in the blanks with the appropriate word. The word form may need changing.

1. The garbage collector was a _____ older man who never had a kind word for anyone.

2. Following the championship soccer match, the stadium was in a state of _____.

3. An elephant uses its trunk in a _____ manner.

4. The running back dashed down the field _____ right and left to avoid the tacklers.

5. The new, tough administrator was sent to take over the hospital which was _____ with problems.

6. One _____ for admission to college is high SAT scores.

7. The sailor pulled the lines _____, so he could sail against the wind.

8. It is _____ that two plus two equals four.

9. Because his parents are such hard workers, Kevin's _____ in school came as a shock to them.

10. Many _____ people became enlightened during the Renaissance.

RESPITE
(RES pit) *n.*
delay; postpone; a brief
interval of rest
Link: **REST A BIT**

*"After pitching a double header, David took a
RESPITE to REST A BIT."*

❑ The condemned man was given a RESPITE to
   enjoy his favorite meal before his execution.

❑ The class had worked so hard throughout the
   semester that the teacher gave them a RESPITE
   before their exam.

❑ Although Ed believed he had escaped punishment,
   when the dean came to get him he realized he had
   only gotten a RESPITE.

PERSONIFY

(per SON i fye) *v.*
to think of or represent as having
human qualities; to typify
Link: **PERSON FLY**

*"Captain Minerich is a PERSON who
PERSONIFIES FLYING."*

❑ Their child **PERSONIFIES** every thing that is good about each of them.

❑ In her poem she attempts to **PERSONIFY** death.

❑ Benjamin Franklin **PERSONIFIES** all the attributes of the Revolutionary period.

FORTE

(for TAY) *n.*
something in which a person excels

Link: FORT

"Steve's FORTE is building tree FORTS."

- ❏ Spelling has always been Zachary's FORTE.

- ❏ Tanya is a born actress, so the director highlighted her FORTE by giving her the lead in the play.

- ❏ Although he loved to play baseball, his FORTE is really golf.

ENMITY

(EN mi tee) *n.*

hostility; deep-seated hatred

Link: IN MY TEA

"Sir Howard, I have great ENMITY for your dog's tongue IN MY TEA."

- ❏ The ENMITY between the teams was apparent to the spectators.

- ❏ When she saw his new girlfriend, it was not easy to disguise her ENMITY.

- ❏ The ENMITY between the feuding families is very obvious in the book.

CRONY
(KROH nee) *n.*
a close friend or companion
Link: **BOLOGNA**

"A BOLOGNA and his CRONY."

❑ Jim and his CRONIES go to the football games on Friday nights.

❑ John Dillinger and his CRONIES robbed the First National Bank.

❑ Edward is honored to be considered one of his boss' CRONIES.

BEVY
(bev EE) *n.*
a group of animals; an assemblage
Link: **HEAVY**

"A BEVY of HEAVIES."

- ❑ Bud's hunting dogs scared out a BEVY of quail.

- ❑ A BEVY of groupies gathered outside to see the star after her concert.

- ❑ While hot air ballooning over the plains of Africa, one may see BEVIES of animals.

BATTERY
(BAT ter ee) *n.*
the unlawful beating of a person; act of beating
or pounding; any large group of related things
Link: **BATTERY**

"BATTERY with a BATTERY."

- ❏ When Joan returned late at night because her car BATTERY ran down, she received a BATTERY of questions from her parents.

- ❏ A BATTERY of artillery on a naval ship usually refers to the entire armament on that ship.

- ❏ After being BATTERED in a bar room fight, Stan was rushed to the emergency room.

ACME

(AK mee) *n.*
the highest point
Link: ACNE

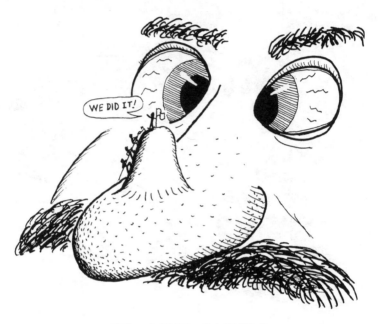

"The ACME of ACNE."

- ❏ Because he thought the stock market had reached its ACME, Mr. Johnston told his stock broker to sell.

- ❏ It had been a hot morning, and the sun had not yet reached its ACME.

- ❏ Lisa thought the story's ACME was effective, but I thought the author should have told more.

PSYCHE

(SYE kee) *n.*
the human soul; the mind

Link: **BIKE**

"The PSYCHE of a BIKE lover."

❑ The study of poetry often helps students to examine their own PSYCHE.

❑ Because the inmate was so hardened in sin, it was hard to imagine that he possessed a PSYCHE.

❑ A true appreciation for classical literature encompasses one's entire PSYCHE.

BANDY
(BAN dee) *v.*
to trade; to give back and forth;
to exchange
Link: CANDY

"Trick or Treaters like to BANDY CANDY."

❑ The doctor said he wouldn't BANDY words; the patient needed an operation right away.

❑ The tennis players BANDIED the ball back and forth until one finally made an error and hit into the net.

❑ BANDYING arms and hands from both sides, Jenny fought her way clear and escaped from the clutches of her admiring fans.

REVIEW #23: Match the word with its definition.

1. respite – (rest a bit)
2. personify – (person fly)
3. forte – (fort)
4. enmity – (in my tea)
5. crony – (bologna)
6. bevy – (heavy)
7. battery – (battery)
8. acme – (acne)
9. psyche – (bike)
10. bandy – (candy)

a. the mind
b. hostility; hatred
c. a brief interval of rest
d. a close friend
e. a group of animals
f. to trade; to exchange
g. the act of beating
h. to think of having human qualities
i. something in which a person excels
j. the highest point

Fill in the blanks with the appropriate word. The word form may need changing.

1. The _____ between the teams was apparent to spectators.

2. In her poem she attempts to _____ death.

3. The tennis players _____ the ball back and forth until one finally made an error.

4. After being _____ in a bar room fight, Stan was rushed to the emergency room.

5. The class had worked so hard through the semester that the teacher gave them a _____ before their exam.

6. Because he thought the stock market reached its _____, Mr. Johnson told his stock broker to sell.

7. Spelling has always been Zachary's _____.

8. Bud's hunting dogs scared out a _____ of quail.

9. Jim and his _____ like to go to the football games on Friday nights.

10. A true appreciation for classical literature encompasses one's entire _____.

267

CHASTISE
(chas TYZE) *v.*
to discipline; to criticize severely
Link: **CHEST SIZE**

*"The trainer CHASTISED John for
his puny CHEST SIZE."*

❑ The teacher began to CHASTISE her misbehaving students.

❑ My mother CHASTISED us for playing ball in the house.

❑ The coach CHASTISED the team after losing a game they should have won.

POLARIZE
(POH luh ryz) *v.*
to break up into opposing factions or groups
Link: **POLAR ICE**

"The Eskimos could not settle their differences and decided to POLARIZE the POLAR ICE."

❑ The issue of what to have for dinner POLARIZED the family; Mom and Sally wanted chicken while Dad and I wanted steak.

❑ The jury became POLARIZED when half thought the defendant was guilty, and the other half thought he was innocent.

❑ The football stadium was POLARIZED into home fans occupying the south bleachers and visiting fans occupying the north bleachers.

TANTALIZE

(TAN tal ize) *v.*
to excite by exposing something
desirable while keeping it out of reach

Link: **SANTA'S LIES**

I'M SANTA. I LIVE IN THE NORTH POLE. I CAME HERE WITH MY REINDEER. I COME DOWN THE CHIMNEY ON XMAS.

"SANTA'S LIES TANTALIZE."

- ❏ The TANTALIZING aroma of the bread made us all very hungry.

- ❏ Jessica would TANTALIZE all the boys with her beauty but would never accept a date.

- ❏ Although the prospect of extra money was TANTALIZING, Joe refused to break the law to get it.

SYNCHRONIZE
(SING kra nyz) *v.*
to occur at the same time;
simultaneous
Link: **SINK**

"The commandos SYNCHRONIZED their SINKS."

❑ SYNCHRONIZED swimming is entertaining to watch.

❑ The captain had his troops SYNCHRONIZE their watches in order to begin the attack at the same time.

❑ One of the jobs of a film editor is to SYNCHRONIZE the stunts so the audience cannot detect where the stunt man took over.

SURMISE

(sur MIZE) *v.*
to guess; to infer (something)
without sufficient evidence

Link: **SUNRISE**

"Run for cover, I SURMISE a SUNRISE!"

❑ Detective Culleton was able to SURMISE the identity of the murderer by the clues left behind.

❑ When everyone began to laugh, I SURMISED that I had been the butt of a practical joke.

❑ Beginning with the very first date, Liz is good at SURMISING how a relationship will turn out.

DEMISE

(di MIZE) *n.*
death; the end
Link: EYES

"The EYES told of Dracula's DEMISE."

- ❑ Chuck was devastated by the DEMISE of his pet turtle.

- ❑ General George Custer met his DEMISE at Little Big Horn.

- ❑ Joe's broken leg led to the DEMISE of his football career.

HIATUS

(hye AY tus) *n.*

a gap or an interruption in space, time, or continuity; a break

Link: **BETWEEN US**

"A HIATUS BETWEEN US."

- ❑ Emily looked to Christmas Break as a welcome HIATUS from the drudgery of school work.

- ❑ Susan asked for a three month HIATUS from work to spend time with her new baby.

- ❑ After reviewing the tax plat, Richard found a HIATUS of ownership between his property and his neighbor's.

EVINCE
(i VINS) *v.*
to show or demonstrate clearly
Link: EVENTS

"EVENTS soon would EVINCE Tom's short-sightedness."

- ❏ The prince wished to EVINCE his love for the fair maiden.

- ❏ The new billboard EVINCED our sales message.

- ❏ Ed spent hours EVINCING the perfect technique of throwing the shot putt.

CRUX

(KRUKS) *n.*
main point; the heart of the matter
Link: **DUCKS**

"The DUCKS were the CRUX of the traffic jam."

❑ After Harry rambled on for hours, it was difficult to understand the CRUX of his speech.

❑ The mechanic thought the CRUX of the car's problem was a bad water pump.

❑ The CRUX of the plot happened just when the suspense was unbearable.

APEX

(AY peks) *n.*
the highest point; peak

Link: **APE X**

"The APE planted his X at the APEX."

- ❑ Our shadows were shortest when the sun had reached its APEX.

- ❑ Christina marked the APEX before she finished the graphing problem.

- ❑ When the swing reached its APEX, we feared the little girl might go over the top.

REVIEW #24: Match the word with its definition.

1. chastise – (chest size)
2. polarize – (polar ice)
3. tantalize – (Santa's Lies)
4. synchronize – (sink)
5. surmise – (sunrise)
6. demise – (eyes)
7. hiatus – (between us)
8. evince – (events)
9. crux – (ducks)
10. apex – (ape x)

a. to break apart
b. to guess
c. the main point
d. to occur at the same time
e. the highest point
f. to criticize severely
g. to demonstrate clearly
h. a gap or break
i. death; the end
j. to excite by exposing something

Fill in the blanks with the appropriate word. The word form may need changing.

1. The _____ aroma of the bread made us all very hungry.

2. Susan asked for a three month _____ from work to spend time with her new baby.

3. The teacher began to _____ her misbehaving students.

4. The new billboard _____ our sales message.

5. The captain had his troops _____ their watches in order to begin the attack at the same time.

6. When the swing reached its _____, we feared the little girl might go over the top.

7. The football stadium was _____ into home fans occupying the south bleachers and visiting fans occupying the north bleachers.

8. Chuck was devastated by the _____ of his pet turtle.

9. The _____ of the plot happened just when the suspense was unbearable.

10. Detective Culleton was able to _____ the identity of the murders by the clues left behind.

278

QUIETUDE
(kwi i TUDE) *n.*
calm; tranquil; peaceful
Link: **QUIET DUDE**

*"Dad was a QUIET DUDE
who sought QUIETUDE."*

- ❑ Gene and Chris chose their property for the air of QUIETUDE and peace that pervaded the area.

- ❑ After the long illness, he had finally found QUIETUDE in death.

- ❑ The QUIETUDE of the substitute teacher took the whole class by surprise.

EXTRUDE
(ik STROOD) *v.*
to force out, as through a small opening
Link: **INTRUDE**

"An INTRUDER gets EXTRUDED."

- ❑ Toothpaste EXTRUDES from the tube when you squeeze it.

- ❑ Black oil EXTRUDED from the engine block.

- ❑ Plastic bags are usually manufactured by large EXTRUSION machines.

OBTRUDE

(aub TROOD) *v.*
to impose oneself or one's ideas
on others; to stick out

Link: **NUDE**

*"Ernie hated to OBTRUDE in the NUDE,
but this was an emergency."*

❑ Ross's OBTRUSIVE parents forced him to attend the same college as they did.

❑ Tanya hoped her parents wouldn't OBTRUDE upon her wedding plans.

❑ Tina's OBTRUSIVE personality made it hard for her to make friends.

ADDICTED
(ah DIKT ed) *v.*
to devote (oneself) habitually or compulsively
Link: **ATTIC ED**

*"ADDICT ED was ADDICTED to
smoking cigarettes."*

❑ My mother's only regret was that she allowed herself to become ADDICTED to nicotine.

❑ His friends worried constantly about him because he was a drug ADDICT.

❑ Betty has become so ADDICTED to soap operas she talks of nothing else.

BRINK

(bringk) *n.*
edge

Link: SINK

*"The mice were on the BRINK of
falling in the SINK."*

- ❑ "My nerves are on the BRINK!" shouted Mom, after our rock band rehearsed in the basement all night.

- ❑ On the BRINK of disaster, Mike finally regained control of the skidding car.

- ❑ Grandpa Ed was on the BRINK of death when the paramedics arrived and saved his life.

EXALT

(ig ZAWLT) *v.*

to raise high; glorify

Link: **SALT**

*"Everyone EXALTED the SALT as
king of the condiments."*

- ❑ The fireman was EXALTED by the press for saving the child from a burning building.

- ❑ Elizabeth felt EXALTED when she scored 1600 on her S.A.T.'s.

- ❑ Our society tends to EXALT actors and sport stars rather than teachers and professors.

HEARTEN

(HAHR tn) *v.*

to give strength, courage, or hope; to encourage

Link: **HEART**

"A HEART patient receiving not so HEARTENING news."

❑ The family received some **HEARTENING** words from the priest.

❑ It was **HEARTENING** to receive so many cards from my friends when I was in the hospital.

❑ Our coach gave a **HEARTENED** speech that made us confident we would win the game.

KINDLE

(KIN dl) *v.*
to cause to burn or ignite; to
arouse or inspire
Link: **CANDLE**

*"Patrick found a unique way to
KINDLE CANDLES."*

❑ Because Christine once had feelings for him, Joe
thought sending flowers might again KINDLE her
affections.

❑ We attempted to KINDLE a fire with candy
wrappers, but apparently we should have used
sticks.

❑ The fire KINDLED when he squirted on some
lighter fluid.

PORTEND
(por TEND) *v.*
to warn of as an omen; forecast
Link: **POOR END**

*"His teacher PORTENDED that Billy
would come to a POOR END."*

- ❏ In ancient times a comet in the sky was considered a **PORTENTOUS** event.

- ❏ The dog let out a howl of dire **PORTEND**.

- ❏ The king believed that his dreams **PORTENDED** some great event, so he went to his sages so they could interpret their meaning.

SEETHE

(seeth) *v.*
to be agitated, as by rage; to churn
and foam as if boiling
Link: TEETHE

"Babies SEETHE when they TEETHE."

- ❑ The class watched the SEETHING teacher take a deep breath before she reprimanded the student.

- ❑ When he learned that his kingdom had been conquered, the king SEETHED with anger.

- ❑ I could see my father start to SEETHE as he started to read the phone bill.

REVIEW #25: Match the word with its definition.

1. quietude – (quiet dude)
2. extrude – (intrude)
3. obtrude – (nude)
4. addicted – (attic Ed)
5. brink – (sink)
6. exalt – (salt)
7. hearten – (heart)
8. kindle – (candle)
9. portend – (poor end)
10. seethe – (teethe)

a. edge
b. to force out
c. to raise high; glorify
d. to give strength
e. calm; tranquil; peaceful
f. to warn of as an omen
g. to ignite; arouse
h. to devote habitually
i. to be agitated
j. to impose oneself or one's ideas

Fill in the blanks with the appropriate word. The word form may need changing.

1. Because Christine once had feelings for him, Joe thought sending flowers might again _____ her affections.

2. On the _____ of disaster, Mike finally regained control of the skidding car.

3. Black oil _____ from the engine block.

4. The grieving family received some _____ words from the priest.

5. The _____ of the substitute teacher took the whole class by surprise.

6. Betty has become so _____ to soap operas she talks of nothing else.

7. The dog let out a howl of dire _____.

8. Tanya hoped her parents wouldn't _____ upon her wedding plans.

9. I could see my father start to _____ as he started to read the phone bill.

10. Our society tends to _____ actors and sport stars rather than teachers and professors.

GASTRONOMY

(ga STRON ah mee) *n.*

the art of good eating

Link: ASTRONOMY

"Sam enjoyed ASTRONOMY, while Big Bernard enjoyed GASTRONOMY."

- ❑ One can learn a great deal about a country by studying its GASTRONOMY.

- ❑ The feast was a GASTRONOMIC delight with every gourmet dish imaginable.

- ❑ In the United States, the winter holidays are the time we practice GASTRONOMY.

PROPINQUITY
(proh PING kwi tee) *n.*
proximity, nearness; kinship
Link: PROXIMITY

*"The Johnson Twins sit in close PROXIMITY because
of their PROPINQUITY."*

❑ Because they were in classes together everyday, a relationship developed based on PROPINQUITY.

❑ The PROPINQUITY of Leonardo di Vinci and Michelangelo is remarkable; the two great artists lived within the same time, at the same place.

❑ Because of the PROPINQUITY of our neighbor's yard, we sometimes hear things we shouldn't.

ANIMOSITY

(an ih MAHS uh tee) *n.*
having a feeling of ill-will;
bitter hostility

Link: ANIMALS IN THE CITY

*"The ANIMALS IN THE CITY showed their
ANIMOSITY toward development."*

❑ The two sisters had a deep-seated ANIMOSITY toward each other.

❑ Displaying ANIMOSITY for his neighbor, Roger built a fence between their houses.

❑ Whenever the two rival teams encounter each other, they show their ANIMOSITY by mocking the other's mascot.

CUPIDITY
(kyoo PID ih tee) *n.*
excessive greed, especially
for money
Link: **CUPID**

"CUPID with CUPIDITY."

❏ The thief's CUPIDITY was exceeded only by his ignorance.

❏ A good politician must have little CUPIDITY but an abundance of caring for his constituents.

❏ The CUPIDITY of the Roman upper-class led to the demise of the Roman Empire.

DEPRAVITY

(di PRAV ih tee) *n.*
extreme wickedness
Link: **CAVITY**

"Dr. Toothkill has a DEPRAVITY for CAVATIES."

- ❑ Ed's mother attributed his DEPRAVITY to violent movies and video games.

- ❑ Muhammad Ali was famous in the ring for his DEPRAVITY toward opposing boxers.

- ❑ The principal could not believe Jason was capable of such DEPRAVED activities.

HIERARCHY
(HYE eh rahr kee) *n.*
categorization of a group according
to ability or status
Link: **HIGH ARCH**

"The HIGH ARCH of HIERARCHY."

❑ Ed was very low on the company's HIERARCHY;
he only delivered the mail and emptied trash.

❑ Chief Sitting Bull was at the top of the tribe's
HIERARCHY.

❑ In the 1700's one's rank in the HIERARCHY of
noble birth often determined his wealth.

PLUCKY

(PLU kee) *adj.*

brave and spirited; courageous

Link: **DUCKY**

"A PLUCKY DUCKY."

- ❏ He fought his disease in a PLUCKY way which we all admired.

- ❏ Her PLUCKINESS made her a perfect candidate for the debate team.

- ❏ Because Roger has such a PLUCKY attitude, we asked him to be the captain of our sky diving team.

GRAVITY

(GRAV i tee) *n.*

seriousness or importance

Link: **GRAVITY**

"Sir Isaac Newton about to realize the
GRAVITY of GRAVITY."

❑ Young children don't understand the GRAVITY of playing with matches.

❑ The GRAVITY of the situation multiplied when Frank made the hole in the boat bigger while trying to patch it.

❑ We didn't realize the GRAVITY of Steven's drug addiction until it was too late.

PATRIMONY
(PA trih moh nee) *n.*
an inheritance from a father or an
ancestor; anything inherited
Link: **PAT'S MONEY**

"PAT'S MONEY is his PATRIMONY."

- ❏ My mother says my overly large nose is a result of PATRIMONY since her family all have small noses.

- ❏ Ill-will in the family was a result of arguing over PATRIMONY.

- ❏ Jonathan squandered his PATRIMONY and died penniless.

CANOPY
(KAN uh pea) *n.*
a covering
Link: **CAN OF PEAS**

"A CAN OF PEAS sleeping under a CANOPY."

❑ The hurricane blew the CANOPY off the garage.

❑ At the beach, Karen likes to sit under a CANOPY to protect her delicate skin from the sun.

❑ We sat quietly under the forest CANOPY and listened to all the beautiful bird calls.

REVIEW #26: Match the word with its definition.

1. gastronomy – (astronomy)
2. propinquity – (proximity)
3. animosity – (animals in the city)
4. cupidity – (cupid)
5. depravity – (cavity)
6. hierarchy – (high arch)
7. plucky – (ducky)
8. gravity – (gravity)
9. patrimony – (Pat's money)
10. canopy – (can of peas)

a. bitter hostility
b. categorization of a group's status
c. a covering
d. the art of good eating
e. an inheritance
f. seriousness
g. brave and spirited
h. nearness; kinship
i. extreme wickedness
j. excessive greed

Fill in the blanks with the appropriate word. The word form may need changing.

1. In the 1700's one's rank in the _____ of noble birth often determined wealth.

2. Young children don't understanding the _____ of playing with matches.

3. The thief's _____ was exceeded only by his ignorance.

4. The feast was a _____ delight with every gourmet dish imaginable.

5. Because they were in classes together everyday, a relationship developed based on _____.

6. Muhammad Ali was famous in the ring for his _____ toward opposing boxers.

7. Jonathan squandered his _____ and died penniless.

8. The two sisters had a deep-seated _____ toward each other.

9. We sat quietly under the forest _____ and listened to all the beautiful bird calls.

10. He fought his disease in a _____ way which we all admired.

300

ACCRUE

(ah CROO) *v.*
to accumulate over time

Link: A CREW

"Pirates know how to ACCRUE A CREW."

❑ Bryan's unpaid parking tickets ACCRUED to the point they would have paid for his college tuition.

❑ By the time he was eighteen he had ACCRUED a good knowledge of computer skills.

❑ The stock dividends ACCRUED so rapidly that we were soon able to buy a new car.

PERPENDICULAR

(pur pen DIK yu ler) *adj.*
upright or vertical; being at right
angles to the plane of the horizon
Link: **PEN**

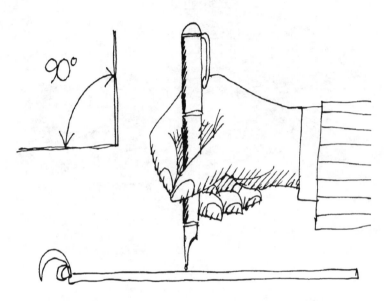

"The PEN is PERPENDICULAR to the pad of paper."

❑ The pole is PERPENDICULAR to the ground.

❑ The tall mast of the sailing ship was built PERPENDICULARLY to the deck.

❑ Because the wall was not PERPENDICULAR, it gradually succumbed to gravity and fell over.

EXEMPLAR
(ig ZEM pler) *n.*
a model or original; an example
Link: **EXAMPLE**

"An EXAMPLE of an EXEMPLARY dog."

❑ Charlie has always been an **EXEMPLARY** student.

❑ The littlest ballerina was cited as being an **EXEMPLAR** student.

❑ Too many teenage girls view fashion models as **EXEMPLARS** for their own body image.

DIRE

(DYE ur) *adj.*

disastrous; desperate

Link: **FIRE**

"A DIRE FIRE."

❑ The hurricane struck the Florida Keys with DIRE results, all the buildings were flattened.

❑ After the girls' wallets were stolen on vacation, they were in DIRE straits; they had no money, no shelter, and not even a quarter to call home.

❑ Jeff's DIRE predictions about a stock market crash unfortunately came true, and now everyone in his family is broke.

GARNER
(GAHR nur) *v.*
to gather or store
Link: **GARDENER**

"The GARDENER GARNERED a large crop."

❑ Maria worked to GARNER all the information she could before she started writing her report.

❑ Throughout her lifetime, Bernice GARNERED enough antique furniture to fill five houses.

❑ Jonathan was guilty of GARNERING illegal information on the internet.

DETER

(DEE tur) *v.*
to discourage; to keep someone
from doing something

Link: **WEATHER**

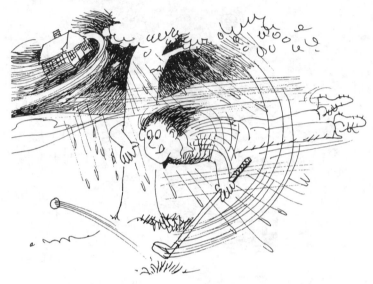

*"WEATHER never DETERRED Jody
from playing golf."*

- ❑ Nothing could DETER John from his ambition to be a doctor.

- ❑ Rachel didn't let her handicap DETER her from competing in the triathlon.

- ❑ Bryan's broken leg DETERRED him from playing softball.

INURE
(IN yoor) *v.*
to get used to something
undesirable; harden
Link: **MANURE**

"Shoveling MANURE takes a while to INURE."

❑ The prisoner became INURED to his new life in prison.

❑ After thirty days at sea, Bob was INURED to life in a life raft.

❑ The substitute teacher was unable to INURE himself to some of the students.

NURTURE

(nur chur) *v.*
to nourish, to feed; to educate;
to train; to foster

Link: NURSE

"NURSES NURTURE the sick and ailing."

- ❏ Mother birds NURTURE their young.

- ❏ Laura NURTURED the abandoned puppy and kept him as her own.

- ❏ During her first year of college, Elizabeth often called her mother for some NURTURING words.

BOLSTER

(BOHL ster) *v.*
to support, as in a group; to give a
boost; *n.* a large pillow
Link: **HOLSTER**

*"Members BOLSTERED each other by
wearing their HOLSTERS."*

❏ The coach saw it was time to BOLSTER his team,
so he gave them a pep talk.

❏ Jane knew she had to BOLSTER the support of
the underclassmen if she hoped to win the
election.

❏ Since Jackie's surgery, she has had to use a back
BOLSTER when she sits.

HAMPER

(HAM pur) *v.*
to prevent the free movement, action,
or progress of; to hinder or impede
Link: **HAMPER**

"A clothes HAMPER HAMPERING traffic."

❑ His small structure HAMPERED Dan's chances of making the football team.

❑ Not routinely changing the car's oil will HAMPER its performance.

❑ A thunderstorm HAMPERED our plans of going to the beach.

REVIEW #27: Match the word with its definition.

1. accrue – (a crew)
2. perpendicular – (pen)
3. exemplar – (example)
4. dire – (fire)
5. garner – (gardener)
6. deter – (weather)
7. inure – (manure)
8. nurture – (nurse)
9. bolster – (holster)
10. hamper – (hamper)

a. to get used to something
b. to support as a group
c. to gather or store
d. a model or original
e. to nourish, feed, educate
f. to discourage
g. to accumulate over time
h. to hinder or impede
i. disastrous; desperate
j. being at right angles to a plane

Fill in the blanks with the appropriate word. The word form may need changing.

1. Maria worked to _____ all the information she could before she started writing her report.

2. Not routinely changing the car's oil will _____ its performance.

3. The pole is _____ to the ground.

4. Mother birds _____ their young.

5. Charlie has always been an _____ student.

6. Nothing could _____ John from his ambition to be a doctor.

7. The prisoner became _____ to his life in prison.

8. The coach saw it was time to _____ his team, so he gave them a pep talk.

9. The hurricane struck the Florida Keys with _____ results, all the buildings were flattened.

10. Bryan's unpaid parking tickets _____ to the point they would have paid for his college tuition.

DOFF

(dof) *v.*

to take off; to remove; to put aside

Link: OFF

"To DOFF is to take OFF."

- ❏ A gentleman should DOFF his hat to a lady.

- ❏ Uncle Jeff always DOFFED his cap at the dinner table.

- ❏ He DOFFED the invitation and promptly forgot to respond.

DON

(don) *v.*
to put on
Link: ON

"To DON is to put ON."

- ❑ Bryan DONNED his scuba gear and dove down to the wreck.

- ❑ Ed took a deep breath, DONNED his parachute, and jumped out of the airplane.

- ❑ As the storm intensified, Bill went below deck to DON his foul weather gear.

SVELTE
(sfelt) *adj.*
slim, slender
Link: **FELT**

"Tina FELT great when she became SVELTE."

❏ The ballerina appeared as SVELTE as an angel as she floated effortlessly across the stage.

❏ One way to stay SVELTE is to exercise a great deal.

❏ The SVELTE waitress was able to move easily between the closely arranged tables.

OBESE
(oh BEES) *adj.*
extremely fat; grossly overweight
Link: **BEES**

"OBESE BEES."

- ❑ Frederick was so OBESE he could not fit through the door.

- ❑ OBESITY is a problem caused by lack of exercise, diet control, and often metabolism.

- ❑ OBESE people are frequently on diets all their lives.

STALACTITE
(stah LAK tite) *n.*
a tapering formation hanging from the ceiling of a
cave, produced by the dripping of mineral-rich water
Link: **TIGHTS**

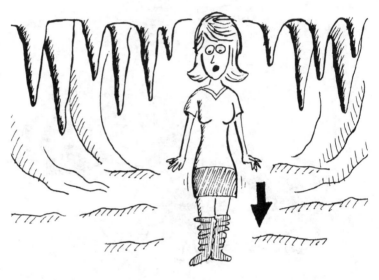

"STALACTITES hang down like her loose TIGHTS."

- ❑ As we worked ourselves through the cave we had
  to be aware of STALACTITES so we wouldn't
  bump our heads.

- ❑ The icicle looked like a giant STALACTITE as it
  grew drip by drip during the winter.

- ❑ Another way to remember STALACTITE is: A
  STALACTITE has to hold TIGHT to the ceiling
  so it won't fall.

STALAGMITE
(stah LAG mite) *n.*
a conical mineral deposit formed on the floor of a
cave by the dripping of mineral-rich water
Link: MITES

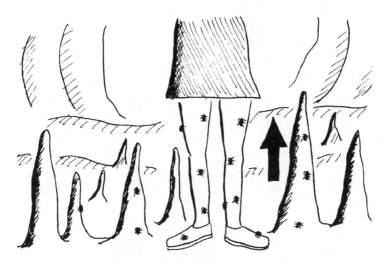

"The MITES climb up the STALAGMITES."

- [ ] The STALAGMITE grew straight up in the center of the cave.

- [ ] It is hard to believe that a giant STALAGMITE was once just a lump on the cave's floor.

- [ ] When our light flickered off, we tripped over the STALAGMITES.

DIURNAL

(dye UR nul) *adj.*
occurring every day; occurring
during the daytime
Link: DAY TURTLE

"A DIURNAL TURTLE."

- ❑ Brad enjoys his DIURNAL cup of coffee while he reads the newspaper.

- ❑ Sunrise is a DIURNAL occurrence.

- ❑ DIURNAL is the opposite of nocturnal, which means occurring during the night.

NOCTURNAL

(NAUK tur nawl) *adj.*
of or occurring at night
Link: NIGHT TURTLE

"A NOCTURNAL TURTLE."

- ❑ NOCTURNAL animals sleep during the day and are active at night.

- ❑ A NOCTURNAL person is one who stays up late at night.

- ❑ DIURNAL, which means of or occurring during the day, is the opposite of NOCTURNAL.

PRISTINE

(PRIS teen) *adj.*

extremely pure; untouched

Link: **CLEAN**

"Marge routinely had her carpets CLEANED so they would look PRISTINE."

- ❏ The coin discovered under layers of ash was still in PRISTINE condition.

- ❏ Those who know about the island keep it a secret because they want to continue to enjoy its PRISTINE beaches.

- ❏ When the archeologists discovered the cave, they ascertained that it was PRISTINE and that they had been the first to examine it.

SQUALID
(SKWOL id) *adj.*
dirty and wretched, as from
poverty or lack of care
Link: **SQUID**

"A SQUALID SQUID."

❑ The house was completely run down, it was amazing how someone could live in such SQUALID conditions.

❑ After the old recluse had died, animal lovers made their way through the SQUALIDITY of her home as they rescued eighty cats.

❑ Upton Sinclair wrote about the SQUALID life of the meat packers in Chicago during the early 1900's.

REVIEW #28: **Match the word with its definition.**

1. doff – (off)
2. don – (on)
3. svelte – (felt)
4. obese – (bees)
5. stalactite – (tights
6. stalagmite – (mites)
7. diurnal – (day turtle)
8. nocturnal – (night turtle)
9. pristine – (clean)
10. squalid – (squid)

a. occurring at night
b. to take off
c. occurring daily
d. extremely pure; untouched
e. slim, slender
f. dirty and wretched
g. a mineral formation which hangs in a cave
h. to put on
i. extremely fat
j. a mineral formation which protrudes from the floor of a cave

Fill in the blanks with the appropriate word. The word form may need changing.

1. The coin discovered under layers of ash was still in _____ condition.

2. One way to stay _____ is to exercise a great deal.

3. A gentleman should _____ his hat to a lady.

4. The house was completely run down, it was amazing how someone could live in such _____ conditions.

5. Frederick was so _____ he could not fit through the door.

6. The sunrise is a _____ occurrence.

7. Bryan _____ his scuba gear and dove to the wreck.

8. _____ animals sleep during the day and are active at night.

9. The icicle looked like a giant _____ as it grew drip by drip during the winter.

10. The _____ grew straight up in the center of the cave.

322

CAPITULATE
(kah PICH uh layt) *v.*
to surrender under certain
conditions; to give in
Link: **CAP PITCH**

*"The Foreign Legionnaires CAPITULATED with a
CAP PITCH."*

❑ After continuous bombing, the enemy finally
agreed to CAPITULATE.

❑ After sending a rose everyday for three weeks,
Betty finally CAPITULATED and married Ed.

❑ The seller studied the buyer's final offer before
CAPITULATING and signing the contract.

VALIDATE
(VAL i dayt) *v.*
to declare legally valid; legalize
Link: **VAL'S DATE**

"Ken VALIDATED himself as VAL'S DATE."

❑ The couple decided to marry and **VALIDATE** their relationship.

❑ The award gave Sue a sense of **VALIDATION** that her work was important.

❑ The parking ticket had to be **VALIDATED** by one of the merchants.

EXONERATE

(ig ZON er ate) *v.*
to free from accusation or blame; to
free from a responsibility or task

Link: HIS HONOR WAS LATE

*"HIS HONOR WAS too LATE to EXONERATE
the innocent prisoner."*

- ❑ When he was released from jail, he finally felt
  EXONERATED for his crime.

- ❑ The general wanted to EXONERATE the captain
  of his war crimes.

- ❑ The man was EXONERATED by a jury of his
  peers even though public opinion was not on his
  side.

EXPATRIATE

(eks PAY tree ayt) *v.*
to exile, banish; leave one's country
(either by force or by desire)

Link: **PATRIOT**

"EXPATRIATING a PATRIOT."

- ❏ Fidel Castro EXPATRIATED many of Cuba's former PATRIOTS who no longer agreed with him.

- ❏ Some American communists EXPATRIATED to the Soviet Union during the Cold War.

- ❏ Ernest Hemingway was one of the first authors to EXPATRIATE during World War I.

PALLIATE

(PAL ee ayt) *v.*
to make seem less serious;
to mitigate

Link: **PAL HE ATE**

"The crocodile PALLIATED for the PAL HE ATE."

- ❑ Christopher was given aspirin to PALLIATE his headache.

- ❑ After Alex's goldfish died, his mother bought him a puppy to PALLIATE his grief.

- ❑ The nurse PALLIATED the patient's burns by applying cold, wet bandages to the sensitive area.

CONFISCATE
(KON fi skayt) *v.*
to seize
Link: **CON CAKE**

"The CON'S CAKE was CONFISCATED."

- ❏ The teacher CONFISCATED Billy's gum.

- ❏ The police raided the suspect's apartment while CONFISCATING all his illegal drugs.

- ❏ The Internal Revenue Service threatened to CONFISCATE the accountant's files if he didn't pay his delinquent taxes.

ELUCIDATE
(i LOO si dayt) *v.*
to make clear and explain fully
Link: **LUCY DATE**

"LUCY, Gary's blind DATE,
ELUCIDATED her intentions."

- ❑ Greg ELUCIDATED his description of the assailant to the officer.

- ❑ Doctors should always ELUCIDATE the medical jargon they use to their patient.

- ❑ Tom Brokow has a gift for ELUCIDATING news to his national TV audience.

INUNDATE

(IN un dayt) *v.*
to overwhelm with abundance or
excess; flood

Link: **IAN'S DATE**

"IAN was INUNDATED with DATES."

❑ After the rains, the fields were INUNDATED with water.

❑ During final exams, we are so INUNDATED with school work that we have no time for fun.

❑ Jack's father used to INUNDATE the front yard in the winter so all his friends could ice skate.

DEPRECATE
(DEP ri kayt) *v.*
to express disapproval of
Link: **DEBRA'S CAKE**

"No one dared DEPRECATE DEBRA'S CAKE."

❑ Josh's parents DEPRECATED his study habits.

❑ The teacher was DEPRECATORY when she realized no one had completed the assignment.

❑ Jerry Seinfeld and many other comics are famous for self-DEPRECATING humor.

RUMINATE

(ROO mih nate) *n.*
to ponder; to reflect upon
Link: **ROOMMATE**

"Larry didn't have to RUMINATE about taking this guy as a ROOMMATE."

- ❏ Because she had made up her mind, Nancy did not need time to RUMINATE when Pete asked her to marry him.

- ❏ The court disregarded the old man's statement believing it to be the product of RUMINATION rather than fact.

- ❏ Michael often RUMINATED about the day when his horse would win the Kentucky Derby.

REVIEW #29: Match the word with its definition.

1. capitulate – (cap pitch)
2. validate – (Val's date)
3. exonerate – (his honor was late)
4. expatriate – (patriot)
5. palliate – (pal he ate)
6. confiscate – (con cake))
7. elucidate – (Lucy's date)
8. inundate – (Ian's date)
9. deprecate – (Debra's cake)
10. ruminate – (roommate)

a. to seize
b. to surrender
c. to make seem less serious
d. to overwhelm; flood
e. to exile; banish
f. to ponder; reflect upon
g. to declare legally valid
h. to express disapproval
i. to explain fully
j. to free from blame

Fill in the blanks with the appropriate word. The word form may need changing.

1. After the rains, the fields were _____ with water.

2. The teacher _____ Billy's gum.

3. The parking tickets had to be _____ by one of the merchants.

4. Christopher was given aspirin to _____ his headache.

5. Josh's parents _____ his study habits.

6. After continuous bombing the enemy agreed to _____.

7. Michael often _____ about the day when his horse would win the Kentucky Derby.

8. When he was released from jail, he finally felt _____ for his crime.

9. Greg _____ his description of the assailant to the officer.

10. Ernest Hemingway was one of the first authors to _____ during World War I.

Review Answers

REVIEW # 1, page 25
Matching: 1-g, 2-e, 3-b, 4-i, 5-h, 6-j, 7-a, 8-f, 9-d, 10-c
Fill in the Blank: 1-voracious, 2 onerous, 3-scrupulous, 4-officious, 5-gregarious, 6-surreptitiously, 7-copious, 8-piously, 9-tenacious, 10-spurious

REVIEW 2# , page 36
Matching: 1-e, 2-h, 3-b, 4-f, 5-a, 6-j, 7-d, 8-i, 9-c, 10-g
Fill in the Blank: 1-writhed, 2-ambivalence, 3-edification, 4-elocution, 5-kismet, 6-ablutions, 7-carrion, 8-pedestrian, 9-pinion, 10-attrition

REVIEW #3, page 47
Matching: 1-c, 2-i, 3-a, 4-d, 5-b, 6-g, 7-j, 8-e, 9-f, 10-h
Fill in the Blank: 1-embroiled, 2-cavalier, 3-ascribed, 4-enhance, 5-deployed, 6-impair, 7-meted, 8-waffle, 9-nullified, 10-egged

REVIEW #4, page 58
Matching: 1-b, 2-h, 3-g, 4-e, 5-c, 6-d, 7-a, 8-j, 9-f, 10-i
Fill in the Blank: 1-abide, 2-diverse, 3-terse, 4-frank, 5-gambit, 6-lithe, 7-coerced, 8-jaunt, 9-abated, 10-aesthetic

REVIEW #5, page 69
Matching: 1-h, 2-d, 3-j, 4-g, 5-f, 6-a, 7-c, 8-b, 9-i, 10-e
Fill in the Blank: 1-abash, 2-gullible, 3-travail, 4-raffish, 5-exodus, 6-influx, 7-mawkish, 8-continuum, 9-languid, 10-intrepid

REVIEW #6, page 80
Matching: 1-c, 2-j, 3-i, 4-d, 5-e, 6-f, 7-a, 8-h, 9-b, 10-g
Fill in the Blank: 1-latent, 2-eminent, 3-incessant, 4-winced, 5-prudent, 6-malcontent, 7-ebullient, 8-eloquent, 9– augmented, 10-diffident

REVIEW #7 , page 91
Matching: 1-c, 2-j, 3-e, 4-d, 5-i, 6-h, 7-f, 8-b, 9-a, 10-g
Fill in the Blank: 1-idyllic, 2-peccadillo, 3-choleric,
4-logistics, 5-dogmatic, 6-emphatically, 7-cryptic,
8-philippic, 9-rhetorical, 10-pandemic

REVIEW #8, page 102
Matching: 1-h, 2-d, 3-f, 4-a, 5-j, 6-b, 7-i, 8-g, 9-c, 10-e
Fill in the Blank: 1-ostensible, 2-succinct, 3-pliable,
4-abstract, 5-accountable, 6-adroit, 7-defunct, 8– baubles,
9-palpable, 10-circumspectly

REVIEW #9, page 113
Matching: 1-f, 2-a, 3-e, 4-j, 5-c, 6-d, 7-b, 8-i, 9-g, 10-
Fill in the Blank: 1-ambulatory, 2-cursory, 3-symmetry,
4-idolatry, 5-ancillary, 6-sedentary, 7-pecuniary,
8-predatory, 9-skullduggery, 10-tawdry

REVIEW #10, page 124
Matching: 1-b, 2-g, 3-i, 4-f, 5-c, 6-d, 7-a, 8-j, 9-e, 10-h
Fill in the Blank: 1-gradient, 2-armament, 3-saga,
4-circumvent, 5-panorama, 6-vent, 7-presentiment,
8-adherents, 9-plethora, 10-corpulent

REVIEW #11, page 135
Matching: 1-c, 2-h, 3-f, 4-a, 5-g, 6-i, 7-j, 8-e, 9-b, 10-d
Fill in the Blank: 1-mammoth, 2-baleful, 3-ethereal,
4-lackadaisically, 5-replete, 6-devoid, 7-atone,
8-diminution, 9-bland, 10-purblind

REVIEW #12, page 146
Matching: 1-i, 2-j, 3-d, 4-b, 5-g, 6-c, 7-a, 8-h, 9-e, 10-f
Fill in the Blank: 1-patriarch, 2-palisade, 3-maladroit,
4-fusillade, 5-cascade, 6-malice, 7-parable, 8-malodor,
9-malaise, 10– paradigm

REVIEW #13, page 157
Matching: 1-e, 2-c, 3-h, 4-f, 5-j, 6-a, 7-g, 8-d, 9-b, 10-i
Fill in the Blank: 1-covert, 2-appease, 3-lampooned,
4-strife, 5-bootleg, 6-boon, 7-brazen, 8-poltroon,
9-conundrum, 10-paragon

REVIEW #14, page 168
Matching: 1-i, 2-e, 3-g, 4-b, 5-f, 6-h, 7-d, 8-a, 9-c, 10-j
Fill in the Blank: 1-eschew, 2-diatribe, 3-lambasted,
4-parley, 5-ransack, 6-camaraderie, 7-offal, 8-escapade,
9-cataclysm, 10-fray

REVIEW #15, page 179
Matching: 1-d, 2-j, 3-g, 4-a, 5-e, 6-b, 7-h, 8-i, 9-f, 10-c
Fill in the Blank: 1-despot, 2-sage, 3-mogul,
4-iconoclastic, 5-nemesis, 6-carnivores, 7-dolts, 8-courier,
9-specter, 10– cloned

REVIEW #16, page 190
Matching: 1-b, 2-h, 3-g, 4-j, 5-a, 6-e, 7-c, 8-d, 9-f, 10-i
Fill in the Blank: 1-supine, 2-serene, 3-Maritime,
4-bovine, 5-bombastic, 6-sublime, 7-spawned, 8-asinine,
9-winnow, 10– forebode

REVIEW #17, page 201
Matching: 1-e, 2-c, 3-d, 4-g, 5-j, 6-a, 7-b, 8-i, 9-f, 10-h
Fill in the Blank: 1-doleful, 2-panache, 3-boorish,
4-fiasco, 5-prodigious, 6-profound, 7-forthright, 8-agog,
9-opaque, 10-forbearance

REVIEW #18, page 212
Matching: 1-g, 2-c, 3-e, 4-i, 5-b, 6-f, 7-a, 8-j, 9-d, 10-h
Fill in the Blank: 1-throng, 2-animated, 3-cataract,
4-annals, 5-elite, 6-booty, 7-barrage, 8-jetsam, 9-tome,
10-portal

REVIEW #19, page 223
Matching: 1-c, 2-h, 3-f, 4-a, 5-g, 6-b, 7-j, 8-e, 9-i, 10-d
Fill in the Blank: 1-torpid, 2-curb, 3-balked, 4-torrid,
5-fettered, 6-mottled, 7-disheveled, 8-nettled, 9-pinguid,
10-prattled

REVIEW #20, page 234
Matching: 1-g, 2-a, 3-d, 4-i, 5-b, 6-j, 7-h, 8-c, 9-f, 10-e
Fill in the Blank: 1-quell, 2-reproach, 3-assail,
4-espoused, 5-dwell, 6-quaffed, 7-estrange, 8-quail,
9-annex, 10-disconcert

REVIEW #21, page 245
Matching: 1-c, 2-h, 3-g, 4-i, 5-f, 6-b, 7-a, 8-d, 9-j, 10-e
Fill in the Blank: 1-reigned, 2-rote, 3-morass, 4-manifest,
5-pacifist, 6-zenith, 7-wrath, 8-bequest, 9-slake,
10-brouhaha

REVIEW #22, page 256
Matching: 1-h, 2-g, 3-d, 4-b, 5-f, 6-a, 7-c, 8-j, 9-i, 10-e
Fill in the Blank: 1-dour, 2-bedlam, 3-prehensile,
4-shunting, 5-rife, 6-requisite, 7-taut, 8-incontrovertible,
9-indolence, 10-benighted

REVIEW #23, page 267
Matching: 1-c, 2-h, 3-i, 4-b, 5-d, 6-e, 7-g, 8-j, 9-a, 10-f
Fill in the Blank: 1-enmity, 2-personify, 3-bandied,
4-battered 5-respite, 6-acme, 7-forte, 8-bevy, 9-cronies,
10-psyche

REVIEW #24, page 278
Matching: 1-f, 2-a, 3-j, 4-d, 5-b, 6-i, 7-h, 8-g, 9-c, 10-e
Fill in the Blank: 1-tantalizing, 2-hiatus, 3-chastise,
4-evinced, 5-synchronize, 6-apex, 7-polarized, 8-demise,
9-crux, 10-surmise

REVIEW #25, page 289
Matching: 1-e, 2-b, 3-j, 4-h, 5-a, 6-c, 7-d, 8-g, 9-f, 10-i
Fill in the Blank: 1-kindle, 2-brink, 3-extruded,
4-heartening, 5-quietude, 6-addicted, 7-portend,
8-obtrude, 9-seethe, 10-exalt

REVIEW #26, page 300
Matching: 1-d, 2-h, 3-a, 4-j, 5-i, 6-b, 7-g, 8-f, 9-e, 10-c
Fill in the Blank: 1-hierarchy, 2-gravity, 3-cupidity,
4-gastronomic, 5-propinquity, 6-depravity, 7-patrimony,
8-animosity, 9-canopy, 10-plucky

REVIEW #27, page 311
Matching: 1-g, 2-j, 3-d, 4-i, 5-c, 6-f, 7-a, 8-e, 9-b, 10-h
Fill in the Blank: 1-garner, 2-hamper, 3-perpendicular,
4-nurture, 5-exemplar, 6-deter, 7-inured, 8-bolster, 9-dire,
10-accrued

REVIEW #28, page 322
Matching: 1-b, 2-h, 3-e, 4-i, 5-g, 6-j, 7-c, 8-a, 9-d, 10-f
Fill in the Blank: 1-pristine, 2-svelte, 3-doff, 4-squalid,
5-obese, 6-diurnal, 7-donned, 8-Nocturnal, 9-stalactite,
10-stalagmite

REVIEW #29, page 333
Matching: 1-b, 2-g, 3-j, 4-e, 5-c, 6-a, 7-i, 8-d, 9-h, 10-f
Fill in the Blank: 1-inundated, 2-confiscated, 3-validated,
4-palliate, 5-deprecated, 6-capitulate, 7-ruminated,
8-exonerated, 9-elucidated, 10-expatriate

Index

Also Available:

Vocabulary Cartoons, Elementary Edition
3rd - 6th Grade
ISBN: 0965242277

Vocabulary Cartoons, SAT Word Power
7th - 12th Grade
ISBN: 0965242285

Vocabulary Cartoons II, SAT Word Power
7th - 12th Grade
ISBN: 0965242269

Attention Schools:
Quantity Discounts on books
Blackline Masters and Overhead
Transparencies are available

For more information and a free catalog
Call 1 800-741-1295

New Monic Books, Inc.
6025 Taylor Road, Unit 4
Punta Gorda, FL 33950
(941) 575-6669 ph (941) 575-6463 fx
www.vocabularycartoons.com